5/06

∂,

Globalization and Human Rights

The New Global Society

The New Gl⬤bal Society

Globalization and Human Rights

Alma Kadragic
President, Alcat Communications International, Inc.
University of Phoenix

Foreword by
James Bacchus
Chairman, Global Trade Practice Group
of Greenberg Traurig, Professional Association

Introduction by
Ilan Alon, Ph.D.
Crummer Graduate School of Business
Rollins College

CHELSEA HOUSE
P U B L I S H E R S
A Haights Cross Communications Company ®
Philadelphia

COVER: Crowds wave banners at Wembley Stadium during a concert supporting South African leader Nelson Mandela on April 16, 1990.

CHELSEA HOUSE PUBLISHERS

VP, NEW PRODUCT DEVELOPMENT Sally Cheney
DIRECTOR OF PRODUCTION Kim Shinners
CREATIVE MANAGER Takeshi Takahashi
MANUFACTURING MANAGER Diann Grasse

Staff for GLOBALIZATION AND HUMAN RIGHTS

EXECUTIVE EDITOR Lee Marcott
EDITORIAL ASSISTANT Carla Greenberg
PRODUCTION EDITOR Noelle Nardone
PHOTO EDITOR Sarah Bloom
SERIES AND COVER DESIGNER Keith Trego
LAYOUT 21st Century Publishing and Communications, Inc.

Library of Congress Cataloging-in-Publication Data

Kadragic, Alma.
   Globalization and human rights/ by Alma Kadragic.
      p. cm.—(The new global society)
   Includes bibliographical references and index.
   ISBN 0-7910-8190-7 (hard cover)
   1. Human rights. 2. Globalization. I. Title. II. Series.
JC571.K28 2005
323—dc22
                                        2005009590

Contents

Foreword

by James Bacchus

IT'S A SMALL WORLD AFTER ALL

One reason that I know this is true is because I have a daughter who adores Walt Disney World in my hometown of Orlando, Florida. When Jamey was small, she and I would go to Walt Disney World together. We would stand together in a long line waiting to ride her very favorite ride—"Small World." We would stand together in those long lines over and over again.

Jamey is in high school now, but, of course, she still adores Walt Disney World, and she and I still stand together from time to time in those same long lines—because she never tires of seeing "Small World." She is not alone. Seemingly endless lines of children have stood waiting for that same ride through the years, hand in hand with their parents, waiting for the chance to take the winding boat ride through Disney's "Small World. " When their chance has come, they have seen the vast variety of the world in which we live unfold along the winding way as it appears to the child in all of us. Hundreds of dancing dolls adorn an array of diverse and exotic settings from around the world. In the echoing voice of a song they sing together— over and over again—they remind all those along for the ride that ours is a world of laughter, a world of tears, a world of hopes, and a world of fears.

And so it is. So it appears when we are children, and so it surely appears when we put childhood behind us and try to assume our new roles as "grown-ups" in what is supposed to be the adult world. The laughter, the tears, the hopes, the fears, are all still there in a world that, to our grown-up eyes, keeps getting smaller every day. And, even when we are no longer children, even when we are now grown-ups, we don't really know what to do about it.

The grown-up name for our small world is "globalization." Our globalizing world is getting smaller every day. Economically and otherwise, our world is becoming a place where we all seem to be taking the same ride. Advances in information, transportation, and many other technologies are making distance disappear, and are making next-door neighbors of all of us, whatever our nationality, whatever our costume, whatever the song we sing.

When Walt Disney first introduced the "Small World" ride at the World's Fair in New York in 1964, I was in high school, and we could still pretend that, although the world was getting smaller, it still consisted of many different places. But nomore. The other day, I took a handheld device, called a "BlackBerry," out of my pocket and e-mailed instructions to a colleague in my law firm regarding a pending legal matter. I was on a train in the Bavarian mountains in Germany, while my colleague was thousands of miles away in the United States. In effect, we were in the same small place.

This is just one example of our ever-smaller world. And, however small it seems to me in my middle age, and however smaller it may become in my lifetime, it is likely to shrink all the more for my daughter Jamey and for every other young American attending high school today.

Hence, we announce this new series of books for high school students on some of the results of globalization. These results inspire hope, shown in the efforts of so many around the world to respond to the challenges posed by

globalization by making international laws, building international institutions, and seeking new ways to live and work
together in our smaller world. Those results also inspire
fear, as evidenced by streets filled with anti-globalization
protesters in Seattle, London, and other globalized cities
around the world.

It is hard to tell truth from fiction in assessing the results of
globalization. The six volumes in this series help us to do so.
Does globalization promote worldwide economic development, or does it hinder it? Does it reduce poverty, or does it
increase it? Does it enhance culture, or does it harm it? Does
it advance the cause of human rights, or does it impede it?
Does it serve the cause of workers' rights, or does it slow it?
Does it help the environment, or does it hurt it? These are the
important questions posed in these volumes. The hope is that
in asking these questions the series will help young people
find answers to them that will prove to be better than those
found thus far by "grown-ups."

I have had the privilege of trying to begin the process of
finding some of these answers. I have helped negotiate international trade agreements for the United States. I have served
as a member of the Congress of the United States. I have been
one of seven jurists worldwide on the court of final appeal
that helps the 148 countries that are Members of the World
Trade Organization to uphold international trade rules and
to peacefully resolve international trade disputes. I am one of
these who see far more reason for hope than for fear in the
process of globalization.

I believe we will all be more likely to see globalization in this
way if we recall the faces of the dancing dolls in Disney's
"Small World." Thos dolls are from many different countries.
They wear many different costumes. But their faces are very
much the same. The song they sing is the same. And, in that
song, they remind us all that as we all ride together, "There's so

much that we share, that it's time we're aware it's a small world, after all." Indeed it is. And, if we remember all that we in the world share—if we remember above all, our shared humanity—then we will be much more likely to make globalization a reason to hope that our smaller world will also be a better world.

James Bacchus
Chairman, Global Trade Practice Group
of Greenberg Traurig, P.A.
April 2005

Introduction
by Ilan Alon

Globalization is now an omnipresent phenomenon in society, economics, and politics, affecting industry and government, and all other walks of life in one form or another. THE NEW GLOBAL SOCIETY series gives the reader a well-rounded understanding of the forces of globalization and its multifaceted impact on our world. The international flavor is evident in the make-up of the authors in the series, who include one Israeli, one New Zealander, one Bulgarian, one Korean, and two American scholars. In addition to an international slate of authors, many of whom have lived and worked around the world, the writers hail from fields as diverse as economics, business, comparative literature, and journalism. Their varied experiences and points of view bring a comprehensive and diverse analysis to the topics they write about.

While the books were written to stand alone, those readers who complete all six will find many points of commonality between the books and many instances where observations from one book can be directly applied to points made in another.

These books are written for the lay person and include definitions of key terms and ideas and many examples that help the reader make the ideas more concrete. The books are short and non-technical and are intended to spur the reader to read more about globalization outside these books and in other sources such as magazines, newspapers, journals, Internet sources, and other books on the topics. The discussion of the positive and negative aspects of the consequences of globalization, both here and abroad, will allow the reader to make their own judgments about the merits and demerits of globalization.

A brief description of each of the six books in the series follows:

Globalization and Development—Eugene D. Jaffe

Eugene D. Jaffe of the Graduate School of Business, Bar-Ilan University, Israel, and current Visiting Professor at Copenhagen Business School, Denmark, explains the key terms and concepts of globalization and its historical development. Specifically, it ties globalization to economic development and examines globalization's impact on both developed and developing countries. Arguments for and against globalization are presented. The relevance of globalization for the American economy is specifically addressed in a later chapter.

There are many illustrations of the concepts through stories and case examples, photographs, tables, and diagrams After reading this book, students should have a good understanding of the positive and negative aspects of globalization and will be better able to understand the issues as they appear in the press and other media.

Globalization and Labor—Peter Enderwick

Peter Enderwick is Professor of International Business, Auckland University of Technology, New Zealand, and a long-time researcher on international labor issues. His book provides a discussion of the impact of globalization on labor with a focus on employment, earnings, staffing strategies, and human resource management within global business. Contemporary issues and concerns such as offshore sourcing, labor standards, decreasing social mobility, and income inequality are treated. The book contains many case examples and vignettes illustrating that while globalization creates both winners and losers, there are opportunities to increase the beneficial effects through appropriate policy.

Globalization and Poverty—Nadejda Ballard

Nadejda Ballard is a professional international business consultant with clients in the United States and Europe and is an adjunct instructor for international business at Rollins College, Winter Park, Florida. In addition to her extensive experience living and working in various countries, Nadejda is also a native of Bulgaria, a developing country that is struggling with many of the issues discussed in her book.

Globalization, which is reshaping our society at all levels from the individual to the national and regional, is also changing the way we define poverty and attempt to combat it. The book includes the ideas of academics and researchers as well as those who are charged at the practical level with grappling with the issues of world poverty. Unlike other books on the subject, her aim is not to promote a certain view or theory, but to provide a realistic overview of the current situation and the strategies intended to improve it. The book is rich with such visual aids as maps, photographs, tables, and charts.

Globalization and the Environment—Ho-Won Jeong

Howon Jeong teaches at the Institute for Conflict Analysis and Resolution at George Mason University and is author of *Global Environmental Policymaking*. His new book for Chelsea House discusses the major global impacts of human activities on the environment including global warming, ozone depletion, the loss of biological diversity, deforestation, and soil erosion, among other topics. This book explores the interrelationship of human life and nature. The earth has finite resources and our every action has consequences for the future. The effects of human consumption and pollution are felt in every corner of the globe. How we choose to live will affect generations to come. The book should generate an awareness of the ongoing degradation of our environment and it is hoped that this awareness will serve as a catalyst for action needed to be undertaken for and by future generations.

Globalization, Culture, and Language—Richard E. Lee

Richard E. Lee teaches comparative literature at the College of Oneonta, State University of New York. The author believes that globalization is a complex phenomenon of contemporary life, but one with deep ties to the past movements of people and ideas around the world. By placing globalization within this historical context, the author casts the reader as part of those long-term cultural trends.

The author recognizes that his American audience is largely composed of people who speak one language. He introduces such readers to the issues related to a multilingual, global phenomenon. Readers will also learn from the book that the cultural impacts of globalization are not merely a one-way street from the United States to the rest of the world. The interconnectedness of the modern world means that the movements of ideas and people affect everyone.

Globalization and Human Rights—Alma Kadragic

Alma Kadragic is a journalist, a writer, and an adjunct professor at Phoenix University. She was a writer and producer for ABC News in New York, Washington D.C., and London for 16 years. From 1983-89 she was ABC News bureau chief in Warsaw, Poland, and led news coverage of the events that led to the fall of Communism in Poland, Hungary, Czechoslovakia, East Germany, and Yugoslavia.

Her book links two of the fundamental issues of our time: globalization and human rights. Human rights are the foundation on which the United States was establised in the late

18th century. Today, guarantees of basic human rights are included in the constitutions of most countries.

The author examines the challenges and opportunities globalization presents for the development of human rights in many countries. Globalization often brings changes to the way people live. Sometimes these changes expand human rights, but sometimes they threaten them. Both the positive and negative impacts of globalization on personal freedom and other measures of human rights are examined. It also considers how the globalization of the mass media can work to protect the human rights of individuals in any country.

All of the books in THE NEW GLOBAL SOCIETY series examine both the pros and the cons of the consequences of globalization in an objective manner. Taken together they provide the readers with a concise and readable introduction to one of the most pervasive and fascinating phenomena of our time.

Dr. Ilan Alon
Crummer Graduate School of Business
Rollins College
April 2005

The Human Face
of Globalization

A bottle of bottled water held 30 little turtles. It didn't matter that each turtle had to rattle a metal ladle in order to get a little bit of noodles, a total turtle delicacy. The problem was that there were many turtle battles for less than oodles of noodles.[1]

30 Little Turtles and Oodles of Noodles

At 24/7 Customer, a call center in Bangalore, India, a number of 20-year-olds are learning to make their English more under-standable to British, American, and Canadian clients. A visiting American, *New York Times* columnist Thomas Friedman, is asked to read the passage about the little turtles—a tongue twister like "Peter Piper picked a peck of pickled peppers" but presenting special problems because of the way people speak English in India—so that the young Indians can hear how it should sound from a North American. They're getting on the job training in what is called "accent neutralization."[2]

After hearing the visitor read the turtle passage, the young people take turns reading it, struggling to soften their harder sounds and slowing down to get through all those urtle, attle, and oodle sounds. Indians tend to speak English faster and in a choppier way than North Americans, so they have to work at drawling, extending the sounds, and slowing down. Every so often one of the listeners starts laughing, and sometimes the one concentrating hard to get through the words breaks up and has to start over again. They're having fun, but what they're doing is not just fun and games. Learning to pronounce English so that Americans and Canadians can understand it is a requirement for keeping their jobs.[3]

Source: Thomas L. Friedman, "30 Little Turtles," The New York Times, February 29, 2004.

If these young Indian workers were providing customer service and answering help desk questions for a company in India, their kind of English would be perfectly understandable to whoever might call. But 24/7 Customer, their company, is one of many in India that offer remote customer service and help desk functions for clients outside of India, in the United States, Canada, United Kingdom, and Australia—wherever English is the common language. Having employees who can communicate effectively with people in another country is essential for the survival of 24/7 Customer. Similar providers of remote services can be found in other countries, such as the Philippines, Malaysia, and Bulgaria, where education in English has been emphasized.

Figure 1.1 These are Indian employees working at a call center in Bangalore, India. India's call centers are staffed with English-speaking workers paid a fraction of the wage they would command in the United States. They provide customer service help lines for companies around the world.

LONG-DISTANCE QUESTIONS AND ANSWERS

Until recently, no one would have dreamed that people thousands of miles away in another country could answer questions from customers at home. However, with fast and reliable international phone service in many parts of the world and access to the Internet, activities that once had to be performed on site or next door can be done on the next continent. In fact, when someone dials a toll-free number, and after going through voicemail reaches a human ready to help, the location of that human isn't generally an issue. It doesn't matter if the person is in the same city as the caller or across the world. The only consideration is whether the person can solve the problem.

The use of call centers like 24/7 Customer in India and similar operations in other countries is an example of globalization, in which companies use the entire world for their labor rather than just the portion that is the home country (Figure 1.1).

Globalization, in this case finding the best place to perform a certain business function regardless of where it might be, is the reason why young Indians are learning how to pronounce words they already know in a manner that makes it easier for North Americans to understand.

Why would enormous multinational companies like Citibank, Microsoft, and American Express, all of them head-quartered in the United States, go to the trouble of setting up customer service outside their home country? For only one reason: to reduce their costs and therefore to be more efficient. In business, keeping costs level is not an option because competitors are continually moving to capture customers by conducting business at a lower cost.

Businesses are continually striving to find better and less costly ways of handling customer service, one of the most critical, problematic, and expensive areas for many companies. What is cost-effective today won't necessarily be so tomorrow. At the same time, customers are always looking for lower prices and easily overlook loyalty to one company for a bargain offered by another.

For an American business, hiring a company in India or anywhere else to take customer phone calls makes sense only if the Indian company can do it for less than what it would cost the American one to do it at home. According to Thomas Friedman's column, the young Indians wrapping their tongues around the turtle story earn between $200 and $300 per month. Even at the top rate, that's less than some American high school students earn per week from part-time jobs, and it's about one-third or one-fourth less than the starting salary for someone who works full time in a call center in the United States.

To the American company entrusting its customer service calls to the 24/7 Customer, the cost of labor isn't the only financial consideration. Wherever they operate, American companies have taxes to pay and bureaucratic hoops to jump through. If it becomes more expensive and slower than doing the job at home, no company will go to the trouble of taking work outside its own country. But because living standards are significantly different around the world, for many businesses it makes economic sense to move work to a country with lower wages. This process is called **outsourcing**, and it is one of the more visible signs of globalization.

Americans often complain about jobs being outsourced. However, while working in a call center isn't considered a prestigious job in the United States, in countries like India, it is. The young Indians making $200 to $300 a month answering customers' questions are earning much more than they would in jobs unrelated to globalization. Working at a call center and answering questions for Americans and Canadians brings with it some of the benefits of a middle-class lifestyle. Most of these young people are still living at home with their parents. Their new income makes it possible for them to move out on their own and buy some of the consumer goods that most young Americans take for granted.

SELF-ESTEEM PROVIDES MOTIVATION

The self-esteem factor of these young Indian workers is important too. One of the young women at 24/7 said she gets more than just the money from the work she's doing, including "a lot of self confidence, when people come to you with a problem and you can solve it—and having a lot of independence." A young man added that he feels proud when some of his American callers say they like to hear an Indian voice because they believe Indians are doing a good job at help desks. Another said his role model is Bill Gates, and he looks ahead to "starting my own company and making it that big."[4]

This is entirely different than the attitude many young Americans of the same age might have about working in a call center or another position that is considered to be a dead-end job. Where the Indians feel pride and see opportunity, many of their equivalents in the United States tend to feel they are wasting time and working there only until a better job becomes available.

The self-esteem factor is also seen at the McDonald's or other American fast-food restaurants transplanted to countries with a lower standard of living. In the 1990s in central and eastern Europe, when McDonald's, Pizza Hut, and Burger King began to expand, Americans were surprised to find that jobs at these restaurants were very desirable to young Poles, Hungarians, and Russians, who looked at them the beginning of a career with a multinational company. In comparison to what was available in the food service industry in those countries, young people were excited to be trained in an American corporation while earning a higher wage than offered by most local starting positions.

EXPLOITATION OR ECONOMIC OPPORTUNITY?

Some people criticize American companies that hire outside the country for $300 a month when they would have to pay at least three times more for the same work in the United States. They claim that such companies are exploiting foreign workers. Others point to the general level of incomes in countries like India and find that the young Indians at the call center are well paid for their work and can afford a way of life their peers in India cannot. Does outsourcing exploit workers or give them an opportunity? Is the American company doing the outsourcing a corporate villain for taking jobs out of the country and exploiting foreign workers or a corporate hero for helping to improve the economy of India? The answers to these questions are related to the relationship between globalization and human rights, which is the subject of this book.

WHAT IS GLOBALIZATION?

A simple definition of **globalization** is the trend to a single, interdependent, and integrated world. Globalization in the 20th century emerged with the linking of nations and people around the world through transportation. Fast and efficient global transportation made possible bringing exotic fruits from warm countries to colder countries and producing goods in one country using raw materials imported from thousands of miles away. It brought cars and electronics from Asia to Europe and the Americas. It also sent American software, films, and music to Asia, Europe, and Latin America. Globalization can also be thought of as "a process of integration and internationalization."[5]

In the twenty-first century, the speed of communications—by telephone and the Internet—has accelerated the process of globalization. The world is truly interdependent and integrated when we can conduct voice and digital conversations with any-one, anywhere, at any time. Another definition of globalization calls it "an ensemble of developments that make the world a single place, changing the meaning and importance of distance and national identity in world affairs."[6] This means that the positive and negative effects of bad news spread almost instan-taneously. As the planes hit the World Trade Center towers on September 11, 2001, American stock exchanges dropped and closed, causing tremors that resounded in European and Asian stock exchanges as soon as they opened a few hours later.

ATTEMPTS AT POLITICAL GLOBALIZATION

As the 20th-century world became more economically integrated, it was moved toward political integration. Since the founding of the United Nations in 1945, countries have tried to work together for mutual benefit by agreeing on general principles of civilized national behavior and trying to extend them around the world.

Integration of Europe through the **European Union (EU)**, which acquired 15 new members on May 1, 2004, is the best regional example of political globalization, even though it leaves out Russia and Ukraine, two major nations outside the EU's direct influence. Nonmembers, Romania, Bulgaria, Croatia, and Turkey became candidates for membership as of May 1, 2005 (Figure 1.2).

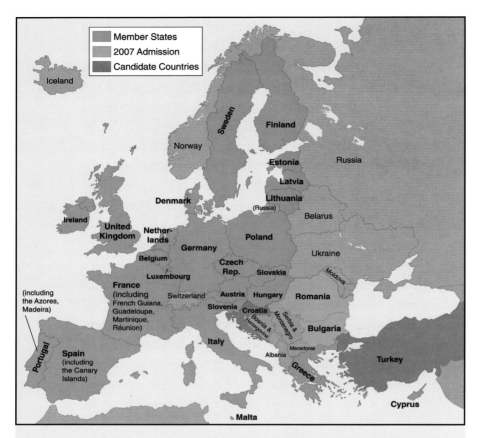

Figure 1.2 The integration of Europe into the European Union is an example of political globalization.

In the Americas, the **North American Free Trade Agreement (NAFTA)**, which encourages free trade between Canada, Mexico, and the United States, is the first attempt at moving beyond the Pan-American Union, a kind of regional UN without much power to influence individual members. Unlike the European Union, NAFTA is primarily an economic free trade zone and is not concerned with political issues among its members or within member countries—unless they affect mutual economic policy.

In Asia Pacific the **Association of Southeast Asian Nations (ASEAN)** is a regional attempt to bring this geographically huge area and its enormous population together on behalf of common interests. However, thus far it hasn't succeeded in setting common economic or political policy, one reason being the discrepancy in size and economic development between some of its members, including China, Japan, South Korea, Thailand, and Malaysia, to mention only the most successful nations.

As a result, while the positive effects of economic integration—as well as some negative ones—are clearly visible almost everywhere in the world, there have been fewer positive effects of political integration. The United Nations has helped prevent some wars and has been responsible for peacekeeping along the demilitarized zone separating North Korea and South Korea since 1952. For many years, it has played a major role in the Middle East in keeping the peace between Israel and its neighbors. It is still active in the war-torn countries of Afghanistan and Kosovo. On the other hand, the UN has not been able to broker a peace agreement between Israel and the Palestinians nor could it prevent the massacres within the past 20 years in Bosnia Herzegovina, Croatia, Iraq, Rwanda, Sudan, and Syria, to name a few of the worst cases.

The United Nations couldn't prevent these tragedies because it is an organization whose members include most of the countries in the world. This means that the country perpetrating the violence sits with the countries trying to prevent it. The UN's General Assembly may agree—even by a huge majority vote—that a country should stop massacring its citizens or should withdraw from the neighboring country it has invaded. But no one can force the outlaw country to obey unless the UN is willing to send troops.

While the General Assembly is the place for nations to discuss their problems, any solution going further than a resolution to support or condemn something has to come from the United Nations' Security Council. The Security Council has five permanent members—Britain, France, Russia, China, and the United States—and several rotating members selected by the General Assembly. No action can be taken over the veto of a permanent member. During the Cold War, many resolutions were stopped by veto from either the Soviet Union or the United States. The UN has no permanent military force; the Security Council has to agree to send a UN force made up of soldiers from various countries. Members volunteer their own soldiers to operate under the UN flag, and this doesn't happen very often. In most cases, the UN can bark but not bite. Political globalization sometimes looks as if it could work, but more often it does not.

POLITICAL GLOBALIZATION AND HUMAN RIGHTS

The UN's inability to step into conflicts affects human rights around the world. The United Nations Charter guarantees human rights to every man, woman, and child regardless of nationality, religion, or race. If the UN is often powerless because strong lobbies form among member nations who are not necessarily interested in human rights, it follows that the UN often can't do much more than talk about human rights. Enforcing them is an internal matter of individual nations.

This raises the question of how to enforce the human rights of an Iranian citizen in his own country when his rights are being violated by his government. If enough citizens in that country are being abused, is that a justification for invading it? The former is one of the reasons the United States gave to explain the invasion of Iraq in 2003, and the validity of the American intervention is still being debated by people in the United States and around the world.

How do you protect the citizen of a democracy whose human rights are violated outside his own country by a non-democratic country? For example, some Chinese-Americans who live permanently in the United States have been imprisoned in China for alleged crimes such as publishing criticism of the Chinese government. In such cases, the U.S. government uses quiet diplomacy, a process that may take years. Because no administration is willing to risk the important trade relationship with

China, the American citizen may languish in prison for some time until the Chinese decide that release makes sense. Certainly the U.S. government or any government in a similar position deplores the way its citizen is being treated, but unless it is ready to take drastic measures, including war to protect its own citizen, what more can it do? It may take the case to the UN where a resolution might be passed, but unless someone is willing to put "teeth" into it—perhaps freezing the offending country's accounts in international banks or denying an international loan—there is no way for that citizen's own country to protect him.

In democracies, human rights are guaranteed by constitutions and laws. They are protected by elected governments that may sometimes stray into abuses of human rights—for example, under the fear of terrorism—and by judicial systems that are usually protected from interference by legislative or administrative bodies. If these protections of human rights don't work, there is always the power of a free press to raise issues and help create a popular consensus in favor of change.

Without democracy, government depends on the will of one person—often a military ruler or a hereditary king—or a party often united by religion, ethnic identity, or a particular ideology. In those cases, human rights depend on whims and reactions to situations and are not guaranteed. When the government threatens human rights, protection must come from outside the country, because the country's legal system and the press will be controlled and unable to significantly diverge from the government line.

The freedom to move around without interference in one's own country and from one country to another is another basic human right. However, the right to move internally has often been restricted by law, as it was in the Soviet Union and still is in North Korea. Externally, nations control immigration and even tourism, and can limit the right of non-citizens to cross their borders. Generally, people try to move from poorer countries to richer ones and from political disturbances toward peace and stability. However, many nations are reluctant to accept immigrants, for a variety of social reasons. That is why most nations, including the United States, have quotas for the number of immigrants allowed into the country each year. The fear of terrorism around the world also has made it easier for nations to justify why they control entry into their territory.

THE SCOPE OF THIS BOOK

In this chapter, we've considered human rights in the category of personal political rights such as freedom of expression, freedom from being jailed without cause, and freedom of movement. However, some critics of globalization maintain that human rights include the right to work and the right not to be exploited. In Chapter 2, we will look more closely at how the definition of human rights has evolved and some of the implications of this new definition for globalization.

Chapter 3 considers the relationship between economic independence, globalization, and human rights. In Chapter 4 we go more deeply into the various aspects of personal freedom affected by globalization. Chapter 5 examines global media from television to the Internet and draws some conclusions about how they affect human rights.

Chapter 6 discusses how non-governmental organizations (NGOs) challenge globalization and fight for human rights using the tools made available by globalization. Chapter 7 centers on how the United States is involved in the movements toward globalization and the expansion of human rights. Finally, in Chapter 8 we make some predictions about the future of human rights under globalization.

A Brief History
of Human Rights

The natural liberty of man is to be free from any superior power on earth, and not to be under the will or legislative authority of man, but to have only the law of nature for his rule. The liberty of man in society is to be under no other legislative power but that established by consent in the commonwealth.[7]

The preceding words were written in 1690 by the British philosopher John Locke (1632–1704) in his essay *Concerning Civil Government*. They were revolutionary at the time because they described the rights of the individual as separate from society. Until that time, political theories focused on what rulers should do to best take care of the people they ruled. The ruler's authority sometimes came from religion—the Bible or the Koran—and other times from tradition or because a ruler had more soldiers and could exercise power. If an individual was mistreated at the command of the ruler, the individual could say it was unfair, but he couldn't claim a human right to express himself or herself, or to have a fair trial.[8]

LOCKE'S NATURAL RIGHTS

In other writings Locke expanded on the idea of the natural or human rights that every person receives at birth. However, as a man of his time, Locke focused on defining how government should be organized to guarantee natural rights because individuals would never agree on where one person's rights stop and another's begin. "Therefore, people form societies, and societies establish governments, to enable themselves to enjoy their natural rights."[9]

This is the reasoning behind the Declaration of Independence that stated the American colonists' pronouncement of separation from Great Britain. The Declaration begins with this definition of natural or human rights:

> We hold these truths to be self-evident, that all men are created equal, that they are endowed by their Creator with certain unalienable Rights, that among these are Life, Liberty, and the Pursuit of Happiness. [10]

Locke's influence is also felt in the Bill of Rights, the ten amendments added to the U.S. Constitution in 1791, which combine individual and social rights, sometimes in the same amendment. Individuals have the right to practice religion freely, to assemble with others, and to write petitions to the government if they have a grievance. They may keep guns at home and be safe from unreasonable searches of their home and their documents.

Several of the amendments guarantee individual rights in the legal system. Individuals cannot be held for a major crime unless a grand jury has indicted them. No one can be forced to incriminate himself or herself in court. The individual is entitled to a legal procedure—due process—before being held by authorities, and property cannot be taken without compensation. Finally, in criminal cases, the right to trial by an impartial and local jury is assured.[11]

The importance of Locke's ideas about human rights in creating the template for modern democracy cannot be minimized. However, Locke wrote at a time when it was generally accepted that these rights did not apply to everyone. His ideas helped support the rise of middle-class property owners against the upper classes, but they also allowed inequality within the middle class and didn't apply to other groups. Women, servants, and people working for wages—men and women—didn't have these rights. Slaves had no rights at all, and only in 1807 did Locke's own country abolish the slave trade. It took more than 50 additional years for Lincoln's Emancipation Proclamation, which abolished slavery, to become the law of the land in the United States.

EXPANSION OF HUMAN RIGHTS IN THE 19TH AND 20TH CENTURIES

Although it was not the intention of Locke and the writers of the Declaration of Independence and Bill of Rights to extend the human rights they recognized to every person, people began to use the rights they had to gain others. They copied the language of human rights provided to others to demand those rights for themselves. The revolutions of 1848 in Austria, Bohemia (today part of the Czech Republic), France, Germany, Hungary, Italy, and areas of the Habsburg Empire that did not become independent until after World War I were based on claims for human rights. Locke's writings and the American Declaration of Independence, later extended in the American Constitution, provided the model.

In many European countries and in the United States, few had the right to vote. People who were excluded because they didn't own property used the right to assemble and to petition the government to attend demonstrations and mobilize thousands of others until the right to vote became universal. That's one way that women in the United States got the right to vote in 1920. In Switzerland where change comes more slowly, it took until 1971 for women to be able to vote.

ENDING TRADITIONAL COLONIALISM

Colonialism, the establishment of control of foreign territories, had been a feature of European expansion since 16th century. It was practiced by European states including Britain, France, the Netherlands, Spain, and Portugal in Africa, Asia, and Australasia/Oceania. Some of the colonial empires built by countries lasted into the mid-20th century. As the mother countries increasingly recognized the human rights of their own citizens, they found it more difficult not to recognize the same rights of the citizens of the colonies. In each case, the colonial powers eventually had to grant the human rights of the colony's citizens, even though they might belong to a different race or practice another religion or come from another social tradition. By the second half of the 20th century, anything that looked like discrimination or suppression of human rights could not be defended for very long. France which had clung to Algeria and insisted that it was an integral part of the French Republic during the 1950s finally agreed to an independent Algeria in 1962. French control had led to a brutal war and broad suppression of civil and human rights. Pressure from the United States and other democracies helped the French decide it was time to let go.

ENDING SOVIET COLONIALISM

Before the mid-20th century, the colonial empires paid lip service to human rights but usually claimed that the colonies were not yet ready for independence and that limited rights were justified by the immaturity of the country. The Soviet Union (as Russia was known at the time) used another approach. The Soviet Union and several of the countries under its influence were among the founding members of the United Nations and thus officially committed to supporting human rights, including freedom of speech and right of assembly.

For the Soviet Union, however, the language of human rights was just words. Every major human right was trampled in the Soviet Union and the countries it dominated from 1945 until the end in 1989 and the collapse of the Berlin Wall. With this turning point, East Germany, Poland, Hungary, Czechoslovakia, Romania, and Bulgaria began the process of democratization, ousting Communist parties, and proclaiming a new era where human rights would be more than a meaningless slogan.

The Soviet empire was brought down peacefully in 1989, because the gap between what it claimed to represent and the truth had become so wide that its leaders—such as Mikhail Gorbachev in Moscow, Wojciech Jaruzelski in Warsaw, and Gustav Husak in Prague—could no longer maintain the illusion that the system worked. People in the countries clustered around the Soviet Union and threatened by its armies had come to know the truth about life outside. Knowing that Western Europe consisted of wealthier countries whose citizens enjoyed prosperity and personal freedom, too many people found that their own poverty and lack of freedom had become intolerable. The restriction of basic human rights was a direct cause of the fall of the Soviet Union.

HUMAN RIGHTS AS A NEW ISSUE IN WORLD POLITICS

Jack Donnelly of the University of Denver is a noted expert in human rights. In his essay "What Are Human Rights?" he points out that using the lack of human rights as a major accusation against another country is rather new from a historical perspective. Before World War II, Soviet mass killings of small farmers in the Ukraine and Turkish massacres of Armenians were not considered by world opinion as violations of the human rights. On the contrary, before World War II, nations were generally free to do whatever they wanted to whomever they wanted within their own borders.

The situation had changed by the end of World War II, when the horrors of Nazi Germany's systematic destruction of European Jewry were revealed, and the victorious allies were faced with the problem of how to treat the perpetrators of the crimes. The United States, Britain, and France set up the

Nuremberg War Crime Trials, which took place from 1945 to 1946 and, according to Donnelly, "introduced the novel charge of crimes against humanity." It was the first time that "officials were held legally accountable to the international community for offenses against individual citizens, not states, and individuals who in many cases were nationals, not foreigners."[12] In the middle of the Nuremberg Trials, 51 nations ratified the Charter of the United Nations on October 24, 1945, setting up a new organization and providing an international mandate to guarantee human rights.

THE UNITED NATIONS CHARTER AND
UNIVERSAL DECLARATION OF HUMAN RIGHTS

The Preamble of the Charter to the United Nations states that

> " . . . the peoples of the United Nations [are] determined . . . to reaffirm faith in fundamental human rights, in the dignity and worth of the human person, in the equal rights of men and women and of nations large and small."[13]

The Preamble firmly established the importance of "fundamental human rights" for all people and all countries; and it was a prelude to the Universal Declaration of Human Rights, which was adopted by the General Assembly on December 10, 1948 (Figure 2.1). The Universal Declaration provided the foundation for the legitimacy of human rights in the second half of the 20th century, and what it started only increased in importance by the beginning of the 21st century. Coming out of two world wars, the Universal Declaration for the first time in international relations linked human rights and peace in the first two sections of the Preamble.

> Whereas recognition of the inherent dignity and of the equal and inalienable rights of all members of the human family is the foundation of freedom, justice and peace in the world,

Figure 2.1 The Universal Declaration of Human Rights was adopted by the UN General Assembly on December 10, 1948. In many countries around the world human rights continue to be violated—even though nearly all countries signed the UN Charter.

Whereas disregard and contempt for human rights have resulted in barbarous acts which have outraged the conscience of mankind, and the advent of a world in which human beings shall enjoy freedom of speech and belief and freedom from fear and want has been proclaimed as the highest aspiration of the common people. [14]

In the first section above, equal rights are the "foundation of freedom, justice, and peace." That assertion places human rights at the center of all relations between the nations of the world.

The second section introduces the expanded definition of human rights that persists to this day. For the first time, "freedom from fear and want" is associated with traditional human rights. In the post-World War II climate, when a large part of Europe and Asia had been left in wreckage and poverty, the individual was assured of life without fear and that the most immediate personal needs will be fulfilled. He or she is at least to have the minimum food and shelter a human being requires. The Universal Declaration did something entirely new: It linked the right to be taken care of with the right to free speech and protection from an arbitrary government.

ECONOMIC RIGHTS ARE ALSO HUMAN RIGHTS

In the 30 Articles of the Universal Declaration, many additional rights are described. In Articles 1 to 21 the rights are generally similar to those in the Bill of Rights, expanded to include all people without exception. The only concept that would have seemed new to the authors of the Bill of Rights is freedom from discrimination.

However, Articles 22 to 25 establish specific economic rights. In Article 22 it is the right to "social security" and "the economic, social and cultural rights indispensable for his dignity and the free development of his personality." [15]Article 23 specifies "the right to work, to free choice of employment, to just and favourable conditions of work and to protection against unemployment." [16] In Article 24 "everyone has the right to rest and leisure, including reasonable limitation of working hours and periodic holidays with pay." [17] Thus, the Universal Declaration of Human Rights established a number of economic rights, adding them to other human rights. However, stating human rights is one thing, and enforcing them is another. In many countries around the world human rights continued to be violated—even though almost all countries had signed the UN Charter. The problem of enforcement remained.

UN HIGH COMMISSIONER FOR HUMAN RIGHTS

As early as 1946, the UN set up the Commission on Human Rights. This Commission meets every year and publishes reports on violations of human rights in various countries. While its findings are reported in the international media, they initially did not receive much coverage by most of the world news organizations.

However, in 1993 the General Assembly ramped up the importance of human rights by creating a new position, the High Commissioner for Human Rights, with the rank of Under Secretary-General, who reported directly to the UN's head administrator, the Secretary-General. The High Commissioner has the power of publicity. By shining a light in dark corners, and exposing the perpetrators of famine and massacres, the High Commissioner can at least try to shame the country accused of violating human rights into some kind of better behavior. This doesn't happen fast, but the experience of the mid-1980s, when the human rights violations throughout the Soviet empire became widely known inside its borders, shows that even dictatorial governments that try to control information can't avoid public exposure forever.

HUMAN RIGHTS IN BILATERAL RELATIONS

In the not so distant past, human rights violations might be known about—like the Soviet-caused genocide famine in Ukraine (1932–1933) and the Japanese massacre in Nanjing, China (1937–1938)—but in diplomatic relations with those countries, bringing up human rights violations was considered taboo and bad manners. That began to change in the United States during the administration of President Jimmy Carter (1977–1981), when the State Department started emphasizing human rights in relations with a number of countries, both allies and enemies.

In the 1980s the United States and some European countries established observance of human rights as an important topic for diplomatic discussion. During the Cold War, American diplomats in the Soviet Union and other nations in the Soviet sphere of influence made a point of meeting with dissidents while on official visits and regularly brought up human rights violations. While those nations usually protested and sometimes even broke off diplomatic relations, the cumulative effort helped lead to the improvement of human rights for millions of people when Communism ended in Central and Eastern Europe.

NGOs AND HUMAN RIGHTS

The term **non-governmental organization (NGO)** refers to any not-for-profit agency generally formed around a focused set of goals and having no affiliation with any government or business. A number of NGOs have played a significant role in making human rights an important topic in international affairs. For example, one prominent NGO is Amnesty International, an organization perhaps best known for its work helping political prisoners. Human Rights Watch is another significant NGO that issues an annual report every January updating the human rights situation in 70 countries.

The importance of NGOs in human rights has been recognized by the UN, which grants some of them observer status. This means that although they can't vote, they can attend and speak at public sessions. The advantage of NGOs is precisely that they aren't nations, so they are free to investigate and report their findings without worrying about the implications for a particular governing party or for a country as a whole. True, the only power they have is the power of spreading the word and of getting international media to take notice. However, this power is not insignificant in our media-focused world, where news travels at the speed of the Internet. Getting the word out about an abuse of human rights often starts the process of acknowledging and eventually ending the abuse, or at least improving life for the victims.

ISSUES IN INTERNATIONAL HUMAN RIGHTS MONITORING

The United Nations administration and its governing bodies have on their side the tools of moral influence and public relations. In practice, however, the General Assembly consists of 191 countries, many of them jockeying for power and making deals with each other. For example, many African countries support each other as a group above and beyond specific issues. The result is that they often vote together to secure a position for one of their group. One concrete result of this is that the country of Sudan has a position on the UN Human Rights Commission at a time when Sudan is perpetrating the massacre of thousands of its citizens, a situation that has been called genocide by former U.S. Secretary of State Colin Powell.

Other countries represented by the 53 members serving on the Human Rights Commission include China, Congo, Cuba, Egypt, Pakistan, Saudi Arabia, and Zimbabwe, all of which are associated with major violations of human rights. As might be expected, the Human Rights Commission has been at best delicate in dealing with abuses and at worst completely unable to censure its members for violations. Critics believe this proves that the Commission is useless. Others say that because these countries serve on the Commission, they will over time learn to be less repressive and more responsive to human rights concerns. In the next chapter, we will examine the evolution of economic independence as a human right.

Economic Independence as a Human Right

As we saw in Chapter 2, the Universal Declaration of Human Rights, accepted by the United Nations General Assembly in 1948, firmly linked freedom from fear and want to previously recognized and accepted human rights of personal and political freedom. That is an important legal foundation for asserting the economic rights of the individual as a normal condition of international cooperation in the United Nations, in relations between countries, and within every country that belongs to the UN. However, as globalization has advanced around the world, violations of individual economic rights show little sign of decreasing, a situation that is often rightly or wrongly blamed on globalization itself.

VIENNA DECLARATION ON HUMAN RIGHTS 1993
The World Conference on Human Rights, meeting in Vienna in the

first half of 1993, took up the relationship of economic development and human rights. Answering widespread concerns that as nations struggled to improve their economies by privatizing industries, reforming tax codes, and encouraging foreign investment, the individual's economic rights could be overlooked, the Conference focused on placing the individual at the center of economic development.

It called for "urgent steps . . . to achieve better knowledge of extreme poverty and its causes, including those related to the problem of development, in order to promote the human rights of the poorest, and to put an end to extreme poverty . . .."[18] In another section the resolution emphasized: "Actors in the field of development cooperation should bear in mind the mutually reinforcing interrelationship between development, democracy, and human rights."[19]

UN COMMISSION ON HUMAN RIGHTS
RESOLUTIONS OF 1998 AND 1999

Five years later the Vienna Declaration, the UN Commission on Human Rights issued a resolution that reminded the world that according to the UN's own findings, " . . . a quarter of the world's people remain in severe poverty; that human poverty constitutes a denial of human rights; that unguided globalization had helped to reduce poverty in some of the largest and strongest developing economies but had also 'produced a widening gap between winners and losers' among and within countries; and that to create opportunities and not to close them requires better management of globalization, nationally, and internationally."[20]

Following this line of reasoning, the resolution approved a year later in 1999 asked the UN High Commissioner for Human Rights "to take steps to ensure that human rights principles and obligations are fully integrated in future negotiations with the World Trade Organization" and the United Nations Conference on Trade and Development to "focus on ways and means to incorporate human rights principles in the process of international trade policy formulation."[21] Finally, the 1999 resolution asked "civil society organizations to promote with their respective Governments the need for economic policy processes to fully incorporate and respect existing human rights obligations."[22]

As globalization accelerated at the turn of the 21st century, it was more and more accused of promoting individual poverty, unemployment, and powerlessness. Where globalization wasn't actually blamed for these economic problems, it was charged with the task of remedying them.

The International Labour Organization was established in Geneva in 1919 to provide a forum where workers, employers, and governments could work together to maintain and improve standards of employment around the world. The World Commission on the Social Dimension of Globalization created by the International Labour Organization studied the effects of globalization around the world, organized conferences in several countries to learn what was happening, and produced a report published in February 2004 summarizing results and making recommendations. Titled "A Fair Globalization: Creating Opportunities for All," the report stated: "The cornerstone of a fairer globalization lies in meeting the demands of all people for: respect for their rights, cultural identity and autonomy; decent work; and the empowerment of the local communities they live in."[23]

According to the report, "seen through the eyes of the vast majority of women and men, globalization has not met the simple and legitimate aspirations for decent jobs and a better future for their children."[24] The World Commission called for a "minimum level of social protection" against poverty for all people and asks that "decent work for all" be a goal for all countries and for international institutions.[25]

ECONOMIC VICTIMS OF GLOBALIZATION

One of the conferences that collected material for the report "A Fair Globalization" took place in the Philippines, where the high cost of economic development is an everyday issue. A man there said, "There is no point to a globalization that reduces the price of a child's shoes, but costs the father his job."[26] He voiced the local concern about small local companies being pushed out by more sophisticated foreign competitors with higher labor productivity and newer technology.

At another such conference in Senegal, a participant said that African business cannot compete with foreign business. He called the situation "unequal combat which would lead to certain death." He predicted that if Africa didn't begin to resist globalization by imposing trade barriers and controlling domestic prices of imported goods, it could not avoid becoming a "beggar economy," relying on international handouts for bare survival.[27]

The well-known economist and Nobel Prize winner Joseph Stiglitz has pointed out that in many less developed countries, land ownership is concentrated among a few elite families, while the majority of people are sharecroppers. In these situations, sharecroppers do the hard work of farming in return for the right to keep a percentage of what they produce. He notes that while globalization didn't create this imbalance, it isn't doing enough to change it. Stiglitz suggests that land reform would make sharecroppers property owners with the possibility of getting credit for improvements that could transform them into successful farmers.[28] Unfortunately, Stiglitz says, this hasn't happened in enough countries. Instead, "for millions of people globalization has not worked." They are worse off than they used to be with "their jobs destroyed and their lives become more insecure."[29]

In his pro-globalization book *The Lexus and the Olive Tree*, Thomas Friedman notes that some critics of globalization inside countries experiencing dramatic changes come from the middle classes that enjoyed privileges destroyed by the new international economic system. He calls them the "used-to-be's" who had trade monopolies granted by the government, jobs protected by big labor union contracts, or benefits that made working less profitable than unemployment.[30] The former "fat cats" who had cushy jobs in nationalized industries supported by politicians are others who dislike the new world globalization has brought.[31]

Another charge against globalization is that it promotes ethnic hatred and even violence in countries where an ethnic minority benefits visibly from economic freedom while the majority is poor. Amy Chua of Yale is pessimistic about the benefits of economic and political freedom in such situations. "When entrepreneurial but politically vulnerable minorities like the Chinese in Southeast Asia, Indians in East Africa, or Jews in Russia call for democracy, they principally have in mind constitutionally guaranteed human rights and property protection for minorities." Democracy to them means "protection against 'tyranny of the majority.'" [32]

But this is only one side of the story of globalization. In the next section we look at some examples of how globalization has helped individuals raise themselves from poverty or significantly improve their present condition and provide the hope of even more improvement in the future, thereby giving them the freedom from want established in the Universal Declaration of Human Rights.

GLOBALIZATION'S ECONOMIC WINNERS

Working Replaces Singing

When doors that were closed for generations suddenly open and stay open, some of those who couldn't get in before, now rush in. That's the case of the Moscow man who used to spend evenings drunk on the street annoying his neighbors with loud singing. Friedman relates that when it became possible for individuals to own small private businesses a few years ago, overnight the drunk became a respectable citizen, going to work on time every morning. Why? He got a share in a car repair garage and never looked back.[33] Previously, he had been one of the millions pretending to work while the all-powerful government pretended to pay him, according to the joke told throughout the Soviet empire during the communist years.

Source: Thomas L. Friedman, *The Lexus and the Olive Tree*, NY: Farrar Straus and Giroux, 1999. Reprinted with permission.

These days India and China are often considered the prime examples illustrating the benefits of globalization. Friedman, who is a cheerleader for globalization in general, has found many examples of individuals with new opportunities and writes about them regularly in his editorial column in *The New York Times.* Chapter 1 of this book opens with Friedman's picture of young Indian workers who are getting the chance to do much better than their parents by learning how to pronounce English like Americans or Canadians. Their jobs at the call center are a ticket to middle-class life. Some of them are planning to continue their education by working on master's and doctoral degrees. For some of the young women in the group, as Friedman points out, the job may mean they will be able to marry whom they choose rather than their family's choice for them. Economic independence for women is new at many levels of Indian society.

In a column titled "Making India Shine," Friedman presents an even more dramatic example of moving up. Abraham George, an Indian who emigrated to the United States and built a software company that made him a millionaire, returned home to establish the Shanti Bhavan boarding school for 160 children from deprived backgrounds. In doing this, George was attacking one of India's greatest problems, the caste system. The caste system divides the Indian people into different classes and confines them to living exactly as their ancestors did because a person's caste is inherited from one's parents. The lowest caste is made up of the so-called untouchables, who have endured virtual segregation from most of society for centuries.

The students at George's school are all untouchables. He believes that giving these children early exposure to technology and education will prove that they too can benefit under globalization, even though they came from an environment that didn't provide the basics of clean drinking or bathing water or indoor plumbing. George told Friedman, "They are the ones who have to do well for India to succeed." In talking with some of the 8-year-olds at the school, Friedman found they had big ambitions for the future: among the professions they mentioned were doctor, astronaut, detective, and author.[34]

In fact, they may grow up to become "zippies," a term used by a newspaper to describe the new group of young Indians . Zippies are "young Indians who walk with a zip in their stride, oozing with attitude, ambition, and money." The young people at call centers are all zippies, a phenomenon brought by globalization. Om Malik, senior writer for the magazine *Business 2.0*, discovered the term when he returned to India after having spent years in America. He uses it to describe Sharma, a 26-year-old woman from a small town near his old home where, Malik tells us, he and his friends used to go to buy cheap beer. In three years the "tiny town built on a fly-blown cow pasture" has "sprouted" six shopping malls and a skyline. That's where Sharma and hundred of zippies like her now work. [35]

In many countries, people who once toiled on depleted farmland have found new jobs in cities where their next meal doesn't depend on the weather and where they have some chance of doing better over time. Although some of the jobs that globalization have brought are in sweatshops, often in less than ideal working conditions, nonetheless they are many times better than what was previously available on the local labor market. All over the world, including the United States, people who haven't had much—among them legal or illegal immigrants—cheerfully take jobs that others consider too difficult and too poorly paid because these jobs provide an opportunity they wouldn't have otherwise.

Some of these jobs are with multinational corporations that are often criticized for paying too little or tolerating inadequate working conditions outside their own country of origin. However, these same corporations face pressures from their home country to make them behave wherever they are, because consumers in economically developed countries expect good corporate citizenship. Zbigniew Brzezinski, former National Security Advisor for President Jimmy Carter (1977–1981), concludes in *The Choice: Global Domination or Global Leadership* that most multinationals pay more than local companies and also tend to avoid some of the worst labor practices such as employing children.[36] In fact, in poor countries multinationals tend to pay double the normal salary.[37]

In his book *Open World: The Truth about Globalization*, Philippe Legrain describes his visit to a Nike factory in Vietnam (Figure 3.1). Nike has often been accused of using foreign sweatshops to manufacture its expensive sports shoes and clothes. In Trung An, a village near Ho Chi Minh City, Legrain found what looked to him like botanical gardens surrounding six large buildings. Inside hundreds of women "[w]earing protective goggles, masks or gloves where necessary . . . cut, stitch, mould, and glue." The women he speaks with tell him they are happier doing this than when they were working for local employers.[38] Legrain makes the point that it isn't fair to evaluate work in poorer countries by the standards of the richest and most developed ones. He claims that working conditions improve as a country becomes more affluent. For example, he refers to a study that found that where annual personal income is less than $500, up to 60 percent of children aged 10 to 14 work. Where annual income is between $500 and $1,000, a maximum of 30 percent of children work.[39] Legrain argues that even where children have to work, they are better off in a factory than laboring in the fields on sharecropper land. One way or another, poor families in poor countries need their children's work to stay alive. Everyone makes the economic choices they have available. Not everyone has all the options.

Outsourcing Yourself

One person who believes in outsourcing is a 23-year-old American who has joined the globalization revolution in India. Joshua Bernstein left a good job with an investment bank in Los Angeles and came to Bangalore, the heart of India's high-technology industry, to join Infosys

Technologies, a leader in software and computer services. He is one of a number of young people from Europe, Israel, and Japan who are taking part in globalization in India.

Few Americans are among them. Apparently, many Americans tend to identify India more with spiritual rather than economic practices. Bernstein says he meets people who come to India because their guru advised it. "I can't really relate to that," he says.[40]

Although very well paid by Indian standards, Bernstein is earning one-third of what he used to get in Los Angeles. But he's doing it for the experience of initiation into another culture. His boss, Infosys CEO Nandan Nilekani, likes to hire foreigners in India to give his employees a sense of cultural diversity and prepare them for multi-national operations. Bernstein is a perfect example of the economic independence possible as a result of globalization, free to take his education and experience anywhere in the world.

So far this section has dealt with the people whose lives have improved as a result of access to better jobs brought by globalization. There is also another way that globalization helps many people who are not employed in the new globalized economy. In the richest and most highly developed countries in Europe and in North America, Canada, Japan, and Australia, everyone benefits from cheaper products made in China or in other low-cost producing countries. Ben Stein has been everything from a speechwriter to an actor and writes regularly about economics. In a column in the *New York Times*, Stein considers two toasters, one made in China and selling at Wal-Mart for $6.87, the other made in the United States and selling at a kitchen products boutique for $49.99. Most people would buy the cheaper toaster at Wal-Mart to save more than $43. Some people might prefer shopping in the more elegant boutique to the mass-market

Figure 3.1 With some 50,000 employees, Nike is Vietnam's largest private employer, exporting 22 million pairs of shoes annually.

atmosphere at Wal-Mart, and some may care for a more expensive look or design, but, if so, they pay for their preference.

Stein's point is that everyone gains from buying household necessities at ever decreasing prices. Even though there may be some Americans once employed in American factories producing toasters who have lost their jobs when the Chinese factories were able to do the same thing for much less, there are far more Americans—perhaps including some of those displaced workers—who benefit by being able to buy cheaper household products. Globalization takes away, but it also gives back. It not only gives back, it spreads the wealth, in this case, to the Chinese workers who are seeing their standard of living rise because they are working in the toaster factory that exports to the American market.[41] Someday they may be able to afford some of the more expensive consumer products they cannot afford to buy right now.

Globalization and Personal Freedom

Contrary to what many people think, multinational companies usually do not try to interfere in the political or social life of the countries where they operate. Because their shareholders keep up with the news, and any unwanted involvement in another country might have a negative effect on the price of shares, the multinationals like to keep a low profile in foreign countries. They are interested in stability, security, and freedom, so they can go about their business and do better than the competition. Citizens of a country where a major international company has set up a subsidiary often do not understand this line of thinking.

In the early 1990s when Levi Strauss established a jeans factory in Poland, campaign supporters of a popular local politician who always wore blue jeans were certain the company would be ready to sponsor the politician's presidential campaign. "He wears jeans all the time, and he would promote Levis wherever he goes," they told an agency representative working with Levi Strauss. They were surprised that the representative was horrified at the suggestion and didn't allow them to talk to the politician directly.[42] The last thing a multinational company in a foreign country wants is to be identified with any one politician or party. Such companies try hard to remain neutral, so as not to jeopardize their position regardless of which individuals and parties win and lose elections.

Being politically neutral, however, doesn't mean that companies have no effect on the countries where they operate. At the Levi Strauss factory in Plock, Poland, young people living in that mostly agricultural region had their first opportunity to work for an American company. For them, everything from human resources to technology was different. They made the adjustment from mostly non-mechanized farming to state-of-the-art clothes production technology virtually overnight. They worked in better conditions and for better pay than their friends in the area. In addition, they were associated with one of the world's best-known brands—and could buy difficult to afford, desirable clothes at a discount.

Like the young Indian workers at the call center, these young Polish workers suddenly had more money and a doorway to higher aspirations. But it didn't stop there. The positive experience of Levi Strauss in Plock became known in American and European investment circles. Based on what they heard from Levi Strauss executives, other companies, like Citibank and General Motors, began moving to Poland, and some of those already in Poland, such as Cargill—an international marketer, processor, and distributor of agricultural food, financial, and industrial products—expanded their operations. Many Poles, not only the young ones, began sharing the experiences of working for foreign companies. In most cases, they exchanged time and hard work for money and prestige, giving them more personal freedom although—like many Americans—they were becoming too busy to enjoy it.

Despite their intentions to avoid rocking the boat, multinationals have an impact on the countries where they do business. Supporters of globalization and its critics agree on that. The question remains, is that impact positive or negative? A case can be made for both views.

GLOBALIZATION HELPS INCREASE PERSONAL FREEDOM

What happened in Poland has been repeated in many other countries. Generally speaking, the higher the standard of living in a country, the more benefits are realized by its citizens thanks to globalization. Even in the United States, which has led the expansion of worldwide trade, globalization has led to greater gender equality in the workplace, as Jagdish Bhagwati argues in his book *In Defense of Globalization*, because the demand for good managers has opened the door to more women.[43] But globalization also improves the lives of much poorer people in less developed countries. Bhagwati found that in Vietnam the rice farmers who became richer as the country's rice exports grew were able to send their children to school instead of putting them to work in the paddies. Keep in mind that this occurred in a country where 26 percent of children aged 6 to 15 are agricultural laborers.[44] Groups as different as American women and Vietnamese children thus have had more options as a result of globalization.

Indeed, Thomas Friedman muses on the contrast between the young Indians full of hope for the future at the call center and three young men he had met some months earlier on the West Bank in Palestine. Whereas one group was enthusiastic and embracing a dynamic future, the other was depressed and had little to look forward to. "They talked about having no hope, no jobs and no dignity, and they each nodded when one of them said they were all 'suicide bombers in waiting.'"[45] Economic globalization and greater personal freedom appear to lie on the other side of the Jordan River in Israel and do not reach over to the West Bank, isolated by the ideology, history, and politics that unites the young men and the other residents in violence.

In other places, globalization "can free people from the tyranny of geography."[46] As Philippe Legrain has noted, in cities around the world, people eat French, Italian, Chinese, Indian, Greek, and other foods from relatively exotic lands. "Algerians in Paris practice Thai boxing; Asian rappers in London snack on Turkish pizza; Indians in New York learn salsa; Mexicans taste Pacific fusion cuisine cooked by British chefs." Individuals have the choice of tempering their national preferences with their own personal ones—it's not the end of nationalism, but perhaps the beginning of a softer, less potentially violent version, at least for some people in some countries. "National identity is not disappearing, but the bonds of nationality are loosening," is Legrain's explanation.[47]

GLOBALIZATION LIMITS PERSONAL FREEDOM

The World Commission Report "A Fair Globalization," produced under the auspices of the International Labour Organization (ILO), says that globalization has not met the "simple and legitimate aspirations for decent jobs and a better future for their children" of "the vast majority of women and men . . . ."[48] In order to come closer to meeting these legitimate aspirations, the report calls for worldwide enforcement of four key labor standards: "the right to organize and bargain collectively, the elimination of compulsory labor, the abolition of child labor, and the ending of discrimination in employment."[49]

However, there are many countries where the economy does not provide sufficient jobs because of war or civil unrest or because an authoritarian government controls capital and doesn't allow private business to develop. In such countries, where there are far more people ready to work than there are jobs, the labor standards of developed economies are difficult to enforce. These countries supply the millions of people who leave their countries for other countries, either to work temporarily or to emigrate.

The most educated and productive of these workers are eagerly welcomed in more developed countries because they are considered valuable additions to the labor force. This group creates what is usually called a "brain drain," which generally refers to the emigration of highly educated workers from developing countries to developed countries. As a result, the less developed countries lose some of the people they most need in order for individuals to take economic strides forward.[50]

Because of the desire of people to move from less developed to more developed countries, many people fall through the cracks and become victims. Today, as the world's population continues to increase on the way to reaching 6.5 billion, there are also more migrant workers than ever who live and work outside the law, making them easy targets for criminals and exploiters. With globalization has come increased traffic in human beings, including women and girls sold as sex slaves and/or domestic servants.[51]

In order to protect the rights of these victims of globalization, the report has noted that:

> Steps have to be taken to build a multilateral framework that provides uniform and transparent rules for the cross-border movement of people and balances the interests of both migrants themselves and of countries of origin and destination.[52]

With these words the report asks for an international agreement involving many countries that sets out clear principles and regulations for treating migrants. The idea is that how a migrant is treated would not be related to where he or she comes from or where he or she is going to. Everyone would be treated the same everywhere.

In his book *The Choice: Global Domination or Global Leadership*, Zbigniew Brzezinski expresses the same need for an international solution. He suggests that just as the World

Trade Organization (WTO) regulates international commerce, so might a new organization called the World Migration Organization (WMO) "help introduce some common standards" for what today is the "arbitrary and inconsistent handling of migrants." He maintains such a new organization is necessary to make globalization more fair.[53] Although Brzezinski wrote his book entirely independently of the World Commission, the approach is the same.

It should be added, however, that not everyone sees emigration out of poorer countries and immigration into richer ones as a problem. Legrain looks rather at the aging of populations in most of the rich countries and concludes, "[t]hey could benefit from an infusion of young people." All kinds of jobs are available in the developed world, from the menial to more skilled. He notes that half of the nurses in London and one quarter of the doctors are foreigners. At the same time, Legrain denies that legal and illegal immigrants take away jobs and increase the cost of social security and other support systems. He believes, "we should still open our borders to the more needy, the desperate, and the hard-working of the world."[54]

MORAL DIMENSIONS OF GLOBALIZATION

The Dalai Lama of Tibet and the late Pope John Paul II both have criticized globalization for ignoring some members of the world community while greatly benefiting others. They both have recognized the need for economic development in the Third World—the poorest nations of the world—while at the same time insisting that the human rights of its people have to be observed (Figures 4.1 and 4.2).

Speaking in Paris in 2003, at the celebration of the 50th anniversary of the Universal Declaration of Human Rights, the Dalai Lama said, "it is the inherent nature of all human beings to yearn for freedom, equality, and dignity and they have a right to achieve them."[55] He also emphasized that human rights are not limited to people living in rich countries. "The aspiration

Figure 4.1 Speaking in Paris in 2003, at the 50th anniversary of the Universal Declaration of Human Rights, the Dalai Lama emphasized that human rights were not to be limited to those living in rich nations.

for democracy and respect for fundamental human rights is as important to the people of Africa and Asia as it is to those in Europe or the Americas."[56] Unfortunately, due to the existence of repressive governments, the most deprived people have the least possibility of speaking up for themselves. The Dalai Lama

Figure 4.2 The late Pope John Paul II was a critic of capitalism and of the unequal distribution of the benefits of globalization around the world. He repeatedly called for economic development in the more impoverished parts of the world, and always insisted that the human rights of all people be respected.

concludes that it is up to those who have the possibility of speaking out to defend the rights of those who do not.

In fact, he refers to his native Tibet, which is ruled by China despite the Tibetan people's desire for independence, as an example of a country where "unsuitable economic policies have been implemented and continued long after they have failed to produce benefits, because citizens and government officials could not speak out against them."[57] Freedom of speech and democracy are necessary components of fair globalization, but not the only ones. The Dalai Lama goes further in this commemorative speech, explaining that he believes "[h]uman rights, environmental protection and great social and economic equality, are all interrelated." In his view, no one and no country can opt out or pretend not to be involved. "Universal responsibility is the key to human survival."[58]

Globalization also involves religious freedom, a crucial element of human and civil rights. The increase in global information and the increased contact between people in other countries challenges religious groups that try to monopolize the attention of their supporters and control their lives. Extremist Christians, Jews, Muslims, and cults of all types insist on total compliance with their beliefs and total allegiance to the texts they consider sacred. No individual member of such groups is allowed to express or act on personal beliefs. Some groups mandate that women cover their head. Some, like the Taliban in Afghanistan, insist that women be covered from head to feet in a shapeless robe called a burka (Figure 4.3). In all these cases, any woman who dresses according to her own preference can be punished.

In the Middle East, parts of Africa and Europe, and even in the United States, the clash of traditional religious beliefs with the globalized world of the Internet, cell phones, and instant messaging can be seen. Although globalization itself doesn't propound views on religion, its effects are destructive to many aspects of traditional religion. For example, when women covered in burqas or wearing head scarves repeatedly see broadcast images of women dressed western-style clothes with free-flowing hair, they are likely to be affected by them. In some cases, the images of women seemingly free from restrictions may shock. In others, the images may lead the more restricted women to ask why they must hide the outline of their body or hair. As a result,

Figure 4.3 This Afghan women appears in public in a head-to-toe robe called a burka. Women are no longer required to keep their faces completely covered as they were under the Taliban, but many women continue to wear this garb.

the most conservative religious groups object to the freedom that global communication brings and try to limit access to the most contemporary technology.

Ira Rifkin, an American observer of the moral aspects of globalization, contrasts the values of the marketplace with spiritual values. Among the values of the marketplace are competition and the fight to earn money. These requirements of the marketplace may conflict with other values, "including the stability of families and communities and respecting the psychological stability that comes from living in a stable setting." Globalization focuses on short-term material gains and swift gratification. All religions tend to focus on spiritual gains realized over a lifetime and beyond. "[Religious critics of globalization] favor a deeply interconnected world in which the needs of people and the environment come before the needs of multinational corporations."[59]

Finally, some goals of globalization and human rights may conflict with others, the result often being an attack on some human rights in order to preserve others. For example, Alison Brysk of the University of California at Irvine acknowledges the sad fact that freedom of speech is also enjoyed by noxious groups like neo-Nazis, religious cults, and terrorists who may be using it to plan to take away individual and political freedom and even to end the lives of other people. Sometimes local groups beginning independent political activity turn into vigilantes or extortionists. Police protecting someone's property may also be harassing poor people by making them move.[60] Where is the boundary between one person's rights and the next person's? In the next chapter, we focus on the role of the media in defining the boundary.

Global Television and
Human Rights Abuses

During the Vietnam War in the 1960s, it took many hours and generally one or two days before film from the front lines could be processed, shipped by air, edited, and finally shown on network television broadcasts in the more developed countries where most people had access to television sets. Such material usually never reached the millions of people either without access or with only limited access to television because their governments controlled broadcast media and censored whatever news footage was available. Since the 1960s, however, the process has accelerated, sharply reducing the time between event and broadcast. The switch to videotape eliminated time spent processing film. Editing became easier, more intuitive, and, these days, almost entirely digital. Smaller and simpler cameras have made coverage of everything, including events that authorities do not want to be covered, much more feasible.

The result is that—outside of countries like North Korea and Iraq during the reign of Saddam Hussein, where the government controls the production of news and uses it solely for pro-regime propaganda—more and more individuals around the world are able to record and process video. Therefore, it is becoming increasingly difficult to keep human rights abuses a secret. The harsh treatment of Iraqi prisoners held at Abu Ghraib prison in Baghdad came to light when videotapes shot by the abusers themselves were broadcast by CBS and then every other television network in the world (Figure 5.1).

It is a curiosity of life today that human rights abusers and terrorists who decapitate hostages videotape their acts and, in the case of terrorists, make the video available on the Internet and to broadcasters. The power of the media—and especially of video technology—means that the laser light of publicity is seldom far from a violation of human rights. While abuses may come to light, however, that doesn't mean that every abuse is publicized or punished adequately.

HOMETOWN BIAS

There is a tremendous bias in every country toward considering its own news by far the most interesting. In television newscasts, a dull and insignificant local story often gets more time than a major foreign story. News producers often joke that while a single death in the hometown may lead the newscast, ten deaths in another state might not be mentioned. A death in another country is evaluated according to the perceived importance of that country. In America, deaths in the United Kingdom are near the top of the list as are those in Israel and Iraq, whereas deaths in European countries and Africa might not make the newscast. In other words, in most countries, only the most dramatic and tragic events outside the national borders merit television coverage. That leaves the place for showing

Figure 5.1 An Iraqi woman waits outside the Abu Ghraib prison to see if a loved one will be released. American news outlets aired photographs of the abuse of prisoners inside the prison walls in late 2003. Ironically, this same prison was used by Saddam Hussein as a center of torture and executions.

internal human rights abuses on internal news programs. However, if the government censors news media—especially television—or if a climate of fear creates what amounts to censorship, although freedom of the press is part of the law, then internal news programs will not expose local human rights abuses.

Another problem with relying on television to expose human rights abuses is related to the essence of television. Pictures are powerful, but that does not always make them meaningful. The power of the picture sometimes leads to a dramatic video, for example, of car chases or hostage standoffs, even when they are of no significance and might have ended five minutes after the video was shot. In putting together their programs, news producers tend to prefer video that looks like a scene from an action series even when it has no news value, rather than less visually compelling but more important material.

CONTROL OF INTERNATIONAL TELEVISION NEWS

For at least the past 25 years, countries outside the developed world have been complaining that international media coverage is dominated by a handful of giant media companies, all of them American or British owned. These share a Western-oriented approach favoring capitalism over state-controlled economics, Judeo–Christian religious traditions over other religious traditions,

Al-Jazeera Covers the Middle East

The Al-Jazeera television channel was launched in November 1996 by a group of journalists operating from Qatar, a tiny country in the Persian Gulf. As the first independent Arabic station, Al-Jazeera calls itself "free from the shackles of censorship and government control."* This is not entirely true, because nowhere on Al-Jazeera can one find anything about Qatar itself. Although the country has subsidized the channel from the beginning, Qatar is never mentioned on Al-Jazeera.

It is, however, certainly true that the station is not directly bound to any important country, unlike government television channels or government-connected channels in Saudi Arabia (Middle East Broadcasting Centre, Orbit, and ART), Egypt (ERTU/Nile Channels), and Lebanon (LBCI and Future-TV). Journalists from Al-Jazeera have been embedded with American troops in Iraq at various times since March 2003. The new Iraqi government has banished Al-Jazeera at times and reinstated it at others. Although Al-Jazeera is often not a good example of objective news coverage, its news about American troops in Iraq and the Palestinian–Israeli conflict are an important source of information and opinion for many people in the Middle East. Since the beginning of 2001, Al-Jazeera has operated a website in Arabic and English.

---

* About Al Jazeera. Retrieved on February 9, 2005 from *http://english.aljazeera.net/NR/exeres/5D7F956E-6B52-46D9-8D17-448856D01CDB.htm.*

materialistic over spiritual culture, and English over all other languages. In part as a response to this perceived problem, since 1996 the Emir of Qatar has been financing the Arab network Al-Jazeera to provide an Arab-based view of the Middle East.

In turn, to answer such criticisms, CNN, BBC, Reuters, and Fox have in various ways tried to internationalize their news coverage and programs. Increasingly, they have employed foreign nationals in the countries they cover, in their permanent overseas bureaus, and at their headquarters. They are also beginning to broadcast in other languages. CNN established CNN En Espanol in 1997 and has been looking at broadcasting in more languages in the future. The BBC is planning an Arabic language

The staff of Al-Jazeera working in the newsroom of the television network in Doha, Qatar. The U.S. government may see Al-Jazeera as an anti-American propaganda machine, but many in the Middle East see it as providing an Arab-based view of news events.

network for the Middle East and the U.S. government-funded Al Hurra Middle East Television Network went on the air February 14, 2004.

INTERNATIONAL MEDIA AIDS WALESA AND SOLIDARITY

In December 1981, the power of televised images, supported by radio and print reporting, helped keep Lech Walesa in the international public eye when the Polish government declared martial law and imprisoned most of the activists in the anti-communist Solidarity union. After being held in jail for almost a year, Walesa was released. He continued his Solidarity activities from home and appeared regularly in public at Catholic masses in his hometown, Gdansk, and around Poland. Although the government never showed his image on the two official channels and claimed he was only a private citizen, it allowed foreign news crews to follow Walesa and interview him—because Poland at that time was trying to have it both ways. As a member of the United Nations and therefore committed to supporting the Universal Declaration of Human Rights, Poland did not want to risk becoming an international outlaw. Yet by allowing the foreign news media to cover Walesa and remind the international audience that there was more than one political side represented in Poland, the Communist government sealed its doom.

In 1983, Walesa was rewarded for organizing first shipyard workers and then other workers and contributing toward the eventual establishment of democracy in Poland by winning the Nobel Peace Prize. Fearing that if he went to Oslo to accept the award, he might be prevented from re-entering Poland, Walesa sent his wife Danuta to accept the Nobel Prize for him. Western television crews filmed him listening to the radio with tears in his eyes as she thanked the Nobel Academy with a few words in Polish.

The Nobel Prize brought Walesa international acclaim and reconfirmed his importance. After Walesa received the prize, few foreign leaders making an official visit to Poland to meet with the President and Prime Minister omitted the nearly obligatory pilgrimage to meet with Walesa. Pope John Paul II—who visited Poland in June 1983 just before martial law was finally lifted and again in 1987 as the anti-Communist revolution was gathering strength—was the most significant visitor in terms of ensuring Walesa's legitimacy as a leader in Poland and raising popular morale. Although the Communist government tried to insist that anyone who met with Walesa would be prevented from meeting with General Wojciech Jaruzelski, the leader of the Communist Party, usually it backed down, being as eager for the international validation that such visits provided as was Walesa himself (Figure 5.2).

The Life and Death of the Solidarity Priest

Jerzy Popieluszko was a young priest at Warsaw's Church of St. Stanislaw Kostka who began holding a weekly Mass for the Fatherland Sunday evenings while Poland was under martial law. St. Stanislaw Kostka was the church frequented by Warsaw's steel workers, members of the illegal Solidarity union who considered Father Jerzy their priest. Because of Father Jerzy's anti-Communist sermons preached at the church, the Communist authorities surrounded the church with helmeted special police before and after the Mass for the Fatherland.

Father Popieluszko was often invited to hold mass at other churches around Poland. It was on one of these trips in October 1984 that his car was stopped and seized by men dressed as police. His beaten body was found several days later in a reservoir.

The death was attributed to the Polish government, which worked hard to clear itself of responsibility and blamed secret police acting on their own. Unlike what would have happened at that time in any other East European country under Communism, however, the Polish government tried the three perpetrators in open court with international media in attendance. They were sentenced to long prison terms. However, the responsibility of their superiors was never fully clarified. In 1997, the Roman Catholic Church in Poland began the long process to have Jerzy Popieluszko recognized as a saint.

Figure 5.2 Lech Walesa won the Nobel Peace Prize in 1983 for his efforts to organize free trade unions and strikes that symbolized political freedom for Poland.

Because Poland was free enough and disorganized enough that the Communist government could not entirely control access to television images from outside the country, primarily from West Germany, Poles saw with their own eyes that what they had been taught in school about the decline of capitalism and the poverty and backwardness of non-Communist countries was untrue. That realization helped lead to the national elections of June 1989, in which 100 percent of the seats in Parliament not reserved for Communists were won by members of Solidarity.

It must be remembered, however, that Poland was relatively free for a Communist country, and the worst human rights abuses were punished officially and publicized in the national media. The best-known case was the torture and killing of Priest Jerzy Popieluszko by members of the country's secret service in October 1984. Although the top leader who gave the order that the priest be killed may not have been punished, several instigators and perpetrators were tried in public and imprisoned. Cases of this type in other Communist countries were never resolved.

TELEVISION NEWS ENABLES THE CZECH REVOLUTION

The downfall of Communist control of Eastern Europe came after two sets of overwhelming impressions captured in television images. The first was in September 1989, when East Germans who had fled to Czechoslovakia camped in the West German Embassy and then were given passage to West Germany on trains that traveled through the Czech countryside. For the average Czechoslovakian, East Germany was considered the ideal Communist country, strong and disciplined, loyal to the system. The sight of Germans fleeing that system impressed the Czechs. A few of them actually witnessed Germans running through Prague, trying to reach the West German Embassy before the Czech police could stop them; most Czechs saw the video on television where it made an impact.

That impact was reinforced and came to a climax a few weeks later when everyone saw the nighttime burst of freedom at the

Berlin Wall on November 9, 1989, as thousands of young East Germans began taking it down, stone by stone (Figure 5.3). The first big demonstration in Prague took place eight days later, on November 17, 1989. It might not have happened at all had those pictures of young Germans celebrating not been broadcast over and over, virtually giving Czechs permission to do the same thing.

Even in Romania, where citizens did not have unrestricted access to television from other countries, many of them could see stations from Italy and Yugoslavia and knew what was happening to the west. Their own revolution started one month later, in December 1989.

Shirin Ebadi Wins Nobel Peace Prize

Despite the criticism, broadcast news media, especially television, provide some of the best ways to expose human rights abuses and to leap over the borders of countries that allow the abuses and may themselves be the perpetrators. The Iranian lawyer Shirin Ebadi, winner of the Nobel Peace Prize in 2003, was recognized for her bravery in defending families of intellectuals and writers executed by the Iranian government. As a result of her activities, that same government imprisoned her in 2000 for what it called "disturbing the peace."*

Ebadi was the first female judge in Iran until 1979, when the Iranian revolution deposed the Shah and established the fundamentalist religious leader Ayatollah Khomeini as supreme authority. Forced to resign from the bench, Ebadi began working as an attorney. Her human rights credentials were cemented in 1994, when she helped found the Society for Protecting the Child's Rights in Iran, the first independent NGO in that country. Outside Iran, she published reports about human rights abuses culminating in the *History and Documentation of Human Rights in Iran*, published in 1999. Over time, Human Rights Watch and other NGOs became aware of her work, and she became a recognized leader in the field of legal rights, particularly for women and children. Media reports about her activities began to appear, leading to the publicity that made her known to the selection committee and helped her win the Nobel Peace Prize.

---

* "Shirin Ebadi." Retrieved on July 23, 2004 from *http://almaz.com/nobel/peace/2003a.html.*

Figure 5.3 Hundreds of Berliners climb on the wall at the Brandenburg section of Berlin in November 9, 1989, demanding that the wall be pulled down. Thousands of young East Germans began to take it down stone by stone.

OTHER EXAMPLES OF MEDIA IMPACT

Economics professor Jagdish Bhagwati uses Myanmar (formerly Burma) as an example of the effect of publicizing human rights abuses in the media. Whereas at one time other nations in Southeast Asia were reluctant to condemn violations by the ruling military government (which includes the use of children as soldiers), today they join in, and Bhagwati is certain that eventually this universal condemnation will have an effect.

On a smaller scale, Bhagwati mentions the threat by some women's groups in the United States to boycott the Vienna Philharmonic's American concert tour because of the orchestra's policy against hiring women musicians. Without much drama, the Vienna Philharmonic's management acquiesced and hired their first woman musician. The orchestra management knew that the negative publicity spread by American media through images of women demonstrating at concert sites could lead to a general boycott of the tour and cost the company a significant amount of money. Because of the publicity, it became easier for the management to hire the woman. This was a case, as Bhagwati points out, where private actions were more effective than anything the U.S. government might have done— assuming it had been interested in taking on such a cause. No economic or political sanctions were required. The threat to the Philharmonic's earnings was enough.[61]

Torsten Wiesel, Chair of the Committee on Human Rights of the National Academies, has spoken out on behalf of Nguyen Dan Que, one of Vietnam's best-known democracy activists, who has been imprisoned for more than 18 years and was once again jailed in March 2003. Wiesel asked scientists around the world to join in calling for Dan Que's release. Wiesel was counting on their voices to have some of the same impact as his reference at the Nobel banquet in Stockholm in 1981 to Dr. Andrei Sakharov, winner of the Nobel Peace Prize in 1975, who had been imprisoned for criticizing the Soviet Union, and was later finally allowed to live freely in the Soviet Union.[62]

Following that precedent, Nguyen Dan Que was nominated for the Nobel Peace Prize in 2004. He did not win this time, but the media publicity will further pressure the Vietnamese government to release him. Further, his having been named as a nominee already forces the Vietnam government to answer questions about why it is holding Dr. Dan Que.

THE UNITED NATIONS HUMAN RIGHTS COMMITTEE

The United Nations Human Rights Committee reviews reports from member nations about the current state of human rights within their borders(Figure 5.4). Once these reports reach UN headquarters in New York, their contents often become known, especially if a country is being observed for alleged violations. The more dramatic cases are publicized by the international media covering the United Nations. This is one way for news about abuses to spread even in situations when news media within the reporting country are banned from mentioning the subject.

The UN Human Rights Committee also reviews complaints from individuals and makes recommendations. Although the UN usually cannot enforce the recommendations, in many cases the publicity leads to reform within the country being accused. Canada changed some laws affecting Indians living on tribal lands to emphasize respect for tribal culture and to stop trying to make Indians into Canadians of English or French ancestry. The Netherlands changed some social security legislation to increase its fairness. Widowers with children did not receive the benefits that widows with children were entitled to. After a Dutch citizen complained to the UN Human Rights Committee, the law was changed in the Netherlands.

In some cases the Human Rights Committee sends an expert or *rapporteur*—French for reporter—to investigate alleged abuses and return with a report. These reports are made public. Later, the rapporteur often becomes a go-between, negotiating with the government of the country where human rights abuses were found. Although some of this work is behind the scenes, the eye of the media is always present, and information may be leaked delicately to add some more pressure so that eventually the government stops the abuses.[63]

This technique was used successfully in the 1970s and 1980s when the Inter-American Commission on Human Rights monitored Chile and Nicaragua through investigative reporting and advocacy.[64] In both countries, citizens endured human rights vioations from police and military. Currently, in addition to the rapporteurs, the Human Rights Commission deploys special groups to investigate certain abuses such as arbitrary executions and detentions, religious intolerance, violations by mercenaries, racism, and so on.[65]

LIMITS OF INTERNATIONAL TELEVISION

The discussion so far has focused on television and its power to highlight human rights abuses, but, as always, there is more than one side to the story. While CNN, BBC, Reuters, and the others have been accused of favoring the American or British point of view in selecting, producing, and broadcasting the news, Al-Jazeera has been criticized for giving terrorists a world-wide platform. The station regularly broadcasts interviews with Osama bin-Laden and his chief associates; it broadcasts video showing hostages being held by terrorists; and it has broadcast video showing the beheading of hostages. As far as we know, Al-Jazeera did not produce any of this video. Presumably, terrorists or their allies delivered it to the station for airing.

While the western broadcasters are accused of creating news that reflects their image of the world, Al-Jazeera is accused of acting as a conduit for material provided by people outside its organization, people who are on the run from most of the world's police forces and many of its armies. This is a new inter-pretation of the mission of a television news broadcaster. Most major international news organizations consider themselves professionals charged with determining what news merits further exposure and how to produce and package it for

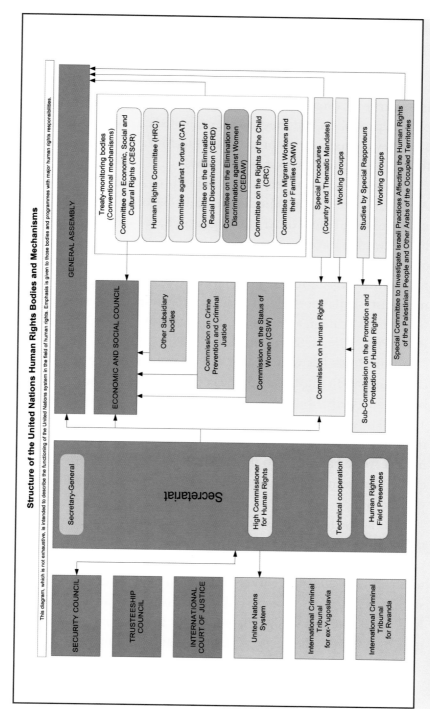

Structure of the United Nations Human Rights Bodies and Mechanisms

This diagram, which is not exhaustive, is intended to describe the functioning of the United Nations system in the field of human rights. Emphasis is given to those bodies and programmes with major human rights responsibilities.

Figure 5.4 The United Nations has an elaborate structure for monitoring and protecting human rights around the world. The position of High Commissioner of Human Rights and the many committees shown in yellow are some, but not all, of the groups and individuals charged with this work.

maximum impact on the audience. As a result, they are reluctant to use material they did not select and produce themselves and use such material only when it has scenes they consider highly important which they can acquire in no other way. This is less true of documentaries, which are often bought from outside producers, but they too are evaluated carefully to make sure they conform to the broadcaster's technical standards and fit with the network's approach to news.

Al-Jazeera has been very successful in broadcasting to huge Arab audiences in the Middle East and beyond. It is only a matter of time before other ethnic groups have their own satellite networks, leaving them free to broadcast material that is offensive to those more concerned with human rights than with nationalistic fervor. To take just one example, promoting fundamentalist Islam is not helpful to developing human rights either for women or men, as was seen in the case of the 2003 Nobel Peace Prize winner, Shirin Ebadi.

Alison Brysk has written that the "character and impact of communication must be analyzed carefully" because the possibility of mass distribution is available to everyone, global heroes and villains. She acknowledges that while mass media make it easier to monitor human rights violations, nevertheless, not everyone has access to the media, and a "digital divide," is created between those who have access to technology and those who do not.[66]

Thus far we have discussed the effect of television on human rights. However, television is a relatively old means of communication that has been undergoing the cycle from new invention to expensive availability, cheaper mass production, and inexpensive necessity. A newer means of global communication is the Internet. As we will see in Chapter 6, it is the primary weapon used by NGOs in their fight against human rights abuses.

NGOs Get Involved

The World Bank describes NGOs as "private organizations that pursue activities to relieve suffering, promote the interests of the poor, protect the environment, provide basic social services, or undertake community development."[67] It divides them into two groups: **operational NGOs** that implement development projects and **advocacy NGOs** that promote a specific cause.[68] The NGOs concerned with human rights are primarily in the advocacy group. They may focus on their country of origin or may be international in scope. The best-known and most effective NGOs involved with human rights are international organizations.

Labor unions were among the first NGOs, and they have participated in the **International Labour Organization (ILO)** since its founding in Geneva in 1919. American labor unions helped lobby to include human rights in the United Nations Charter of 1945. The role of NGOs has developed along with that of the UN. In 1948, some NGOs were recognized by being given "consultative status" with the UN Economic and Social Council. In the 1980s and especially the 1990s, NGOs became important in monitoring human rights and attended UN conferences and commissions dealing with human rights and economic development as non-voting participants.[69] At times NGO access to UN sessions and conferences has been controversial because demonstrators with a particular agenda became disruptive after they entered as part of an NGO's delegation. Security following the terrorist attacks of September 11, 2001, has further complicated NGO access, especially at UN headquarters in New York.[70] However, the influence of NGOs continues to be felt and is to some extent independent of the amount of access to international gatherings. At the turn of the 21st century, *The Economist* magazine estimated that there were 2 million NGOs worldwide and 1 million in India alone.[71]

THE NGO ADVANTAGE

The great advantage NGOs have is that they are independent. It is true that in some countries authoritarian governments try to control them, but in most cases, those attempts fail. NGOs tend to be started by people who want to bypass the standard political process in their own country and in other countries. Therefore, if an NGO focusing on the rights of refugees believes the U.K. should accept more people seeking asylum from African countries, it can act independently of any country's domestic or international politics.

If members of that NGO were to go to the Foreign Ministry of their country or American members were to go to the State Department and demand that more humane treatment of African asylum seekers become a condition of the nation's relationship with the U.K., probably not much would happen. Many countries would be reluctant to approach the U.K. about accepting refugees because they themselves do not accept them. This is certainly true in the United States, where a constant flow of illegal immigrants has made the granting of asylum and immigration controversial and a political hot potato for each administration. During the 2004 presidential campaign, for example, neither incumbent President George W. Bush nor challenger Senator John F. Kerry made immigration a significant political issue.

Continuing this example, in some countries, the NGO members might be ignored. In others they might meet sympathy but also an acknowledgement that the country's relationship with the U.K. is too important to risk on behalf of African refugees. American diplomats might also tend to avoid pressuring the U.K. because Italy is a NATO ally contributing troops in Iraq.

HOW THE PROCESS WORKS

In the United States and elsewhere, the NGO is much more likely to be successful if it avoids formal government channels and instead relies on the informal power of persuasion through the media. To continue our example, by mobilizing its members and using their efforts to create maximum publicity, the NGO has a far greater chance of affecting public opinion and using it to reach the goal of better treatment of, say, African asylum-seekers. Using every format and level of media—local, national, and international—the NGO has hundreds of potential platforms to spread information and influence public opinion. In time, human rights causes taken up by NGOs become part of the political dialogue. Informed people write letters to the editor about it. They call in to talk radio programs. The buzz grows, and politicians notice. Some of them incorporate the information into their own speeches and communications to their constituents. Important media outlets begin to editorialize on the subject. Someone proposes boycotting Italian products. It becomes fashionable to announce that Italy is no longer a favored tourist destination.

At the United Nations, discussions take place in the General Assembly and the Security Council. The Commission for Human Rights sends a rapporteur to investigate and return with an opinion. The report is summarized in a press release from the Commission for Human Rights. Important columnists at major newspapers around the world chastise Italy in their writings. Some editorial boards agree and do the same. The Pope weighs in with a moral condemnation. In Catholic churches in Italy and many other countries, priests ask for better treatment of the African refugees. The Dalai Lama and other non-Catholic moral authorities join in condemning Italy for its refusal to help desperate people. During these developments, which could take several years, NATO country governments need not change their official positions nor ever say anything to the Italian government. At some point, although the Italian government may never officially change its policy, Italy may stop turning away African asylum seekers. The NGO turns its attention to another violation of human rights, and the process begins again.

THE ROLE OF THE INTERNET

Increasingly, the Internet has become the primary instrument for NGOs to collect information on human rights violations, to communicate with victims of violations, to gather and motivate members, to link with supporting organizations, to supply journalists with material, and to provide information to the public. Together over time, these activities build the NGO's credibility, focus public opinion on human rights abuses, and sometimes lead to the resolution of a problem or help ease the abuse. Without globalization, the process would take much longer—if, indeed, the human rights violation ever came to international attention.

Jagdish Bhagwati mentions that when Mahatma Gandhi organized the peaceful gatherings and marches that led to India's independence from the British Empire, he did not have fast and inexpensive means to send messages to supporters. The Internet and e-mail make "organization and coordinated civil action so much easier."[72] The upgraded means of communication brought by globalization allows news to spread in an instant and for supporters to mobilize people and money overnight.

Vermont Governor Howard Dean's campaign for the 2004 presidential election is another example of what can be done by managing electronic communication. It also showed that although the message communicated by the Dean campaign got through, it was not sufficiently popular to strike a chord with the general electorate. Just as Dean came out of nowhere to be the Democrat front-runner for a few months, his campaign faded when it became clear his message turned off more people than it turned on. With or without the Internet, it is difficult to build consensus for a person or idea whose time has not come.

The Internet facilitates the creation of an international lobby for an intellectual position or political stance. NGOs that used to focus on domestic problems within one country saw the potential of joining other groups or expanding their own to other countries. New NGOs with a global focus from the outset were established.[73] Globalization has made possible the maintenance of international networks of people linked by a common approach or a similar desire to fight for the issues they believe in. It has also given small groups and even individuals a way to publicize their ideas in situations where mass media are censored or unwilling to give them a platform. Individuals have websites; they publish blogs, easily updated personal journals that are available on the web; they join discussion lists or chat rooms; they e-mail huge numbers of people. With the Internet, no one can monopolize the media for long.

SOME NGOS INVOLVED IN HUMAN RIGHTS
Amnesty International
Amnesty International (AI), founded in 1961, is one of the most respected NGOs. It has more than 1.8 million members in 150 countries (Figure 6.1). The organization does not accept money

Figure 6.1 Amnesty International was founded in 1961 and today has more than 1.8 million members. In 1977, Amnesty International won the Nobel Peace Prize for putting the spotlight on political prisoners and fighting to end torture.

from any government and is funded primarily by the members. In 1977, Amnesty International was awarded the Nobel Peace Prize for its work to assist political prisoners and fight torture. Each year the organization issues an annual report documenting human rights abuses in 155 countries.

As soon as Amnesty International learns that an individual is in danger of human rights abuse, it alerts members of the Urgent Action Network in over 70 countries. The Urgent Action Network tells its members how and where someone's human rights are being threatened and provides contact information for government officials who have the power to stop the abuse. Network members immediately send messages to those officials. AI claims that in 2004, more than four in ten Urgent Action Network cases saw positive developments as a result of these messages.

Internet Exposure Leads to Prisoner's Release

In early 2005, the Urgent Action web page shows a Sudanese woman named Rehab Abdel Bagi Mohamed Ali who is quoted saying she was released from prison two weeks after an Urgent Action call was issued on her behalf.

"I was beaten and verbally abused in detention. After a few days, the guards asked me, "Do you know that your name is all over the Internet?" After that, I was treated better by the guards before being released. The appeals sent by Amnesty members definitely had an effect on my case."[74]

Derechos Human Rights

Derechos Human Rights (*www.derechos.org*) was the first Internet-based human rights NGO. Derechos means rights in Spanish, so the group's name emphasizes its mission: to promote human rights around the world, to educate people about human rights, to investigate violations of human rights, to promote the rule of law in international affairs, and to assist other human rights NGOs and individuals who have been abused.

The group's primary work has been in Latin America, but it is active in the United States and Europe, too. Headquartered in California with an affiliate in Argentina and a partner, Equipo Nizkor, active in Europe and Latin America, Derechos Human Rights links all of these countries through Internet communication.

Derechos Human Rights maintains a "Human Rights Mailing List" and a "Human Rights Discussion List." The mailing list is divided into sections for human rights NGOs, human rights lawyers, and human rights professionals, and an open forum that anyone can join. The discussion list is open to anyone but is not a forum for attacks on an ethnic group, excuses for human rights abuses, personal attacks, or any kind of advertising. It is also not intended to be the place to publicize human rights violations or issue calls to action for victims.[75] Those things are done through "Human Rights News & Actions," an Internet newsletter that provides current news about human rights abuses and offers archives relating to human rights organized by country and covering most of the world.[76]

The Wall of Memory

In 1976, a three-man military junta, headed by General Jorge Rafael Videla, took over the Argentinean government and began a ruthless campaign against liberals, leftists, and political terrorists. During this so-called dirty war, thousands of people disappeared and were never heard from again. The Derechos website hosts the Wall of Memory (*http://www.desaparecidos.org/arg/victimas/ eng.html*), with photos of 800 people whose families never saw them again. A click on each photo yields a biography and the last known location of the person. On the left side of the web page, a list categorizes the disappeared under such headings as pregnant women, minors, lawyers, artists, and so on.

Freedom House

First Lady Eleanor Roosevelt, politician Wendell Wilkie, and other prominent Americans committed to helping spread democracy and fight totalitarianism founded the organization Freedom House in 1941. The oldest American human rights NGO, it is bipartisan and focuses on producing the annual "Freedom in the World" survey in which countries are rated on civil liberties and political rights. It is something of a maverick among NGOs in that it focuses on changing the human rights agenda of the U.S. government directly, without utilizing its network of members, as Amnesty International does.

Since 1986 Freedom House also includes the Center for Religious Freedom, which monitors abuses of individual and group rights and pressures the American government through direct contacts and through the media. As noted on its website,

> [The Center] insists that U.S. foreign policy defend Christians and Jews, Muslim dissidents and minorities, and other religious minorities in countries such as Indonesia, Pakistan, Nigeria, Iran, and Sudan. It is fighting the imposition of harsh Islamic law in the new Iraq and Afghanistan and opposes blasphemy laws in Muslim countries that suppress more tolerant and pro-American Muslim thought.[77]

Identifying Genocide in Sudan

In July 2004, the Center for Religious Freedom succeeded in getting the Bush administration to define the crisis in Sudan as genocide. For years under the regime of General Omar al-Bashir millions of Christians were killed. However, Sudan has generally been under the international radar, and although many countries denounced the violence, none were willing to call what was happening genocide. According to Center's director Nina Shea, when Secretary of State Colin Powell told the Senate Foreign Relations Committee "evidence leads us to the conclusion that genocide has occurred and may still be occurring in Darfur," that was the first time that a nation acted according to the 1948 Genocide Convention. The United States signed that document and "formally charged another [country] with 'genocide. . . .'"[78]

Global Exchange

Founded in San Francisco in 1988, Global Exchange is one of the newer NGOs. Its mission is to make Americans more aware of global issues involving human rights and to form partnerships with foreign organizations, especially those in the less developed countries. Global Exchange promotes political and civil rights by monitoring violations wherever there is armed conflict and works to improve relations between such countries and the United States.

Unlike Amnesty International and Freedom House, Global Exchange works for what it considers economic justice and generally is opposed to many actions of the World Bank, the International Monetary Fund, and the World Trade Organization. It lobbies multinational corporations to respect workers' rights and protect the environment wherever they operate. Global Exchange has called upon the Ford Motor Company and other car producers to make vehicles that average 50 miles per gallon by 2010. Ford has been targeted because according to the Environmental Protection Agency (EPA), Ford cars are the least energy efficient.

Global Exchange also supports the Fair Trade movement, which tries to level the economic playing field between richer and poorer countries by insisting on "the importance of

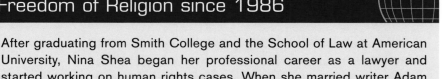

Nina Shea Fighting for
Freedom of Religion since 1986

After graduating from Smith College and the School of Law at American University, Nina Shea began her professional career as a lawyer and started working on human rights cases. When she married writer Adam Meyerson, she joined him in founding the Puebla Institute in 1986. Later it became the Center for Religious Freedom and since 1995 has been part of part of Freedom House. She has fought on behalf of, among others, Christians in Sudan, ChaldoAssyrians in Iraq, and Muslims in Afghanistan.

building a more just global economy."[79] (See the article on pages 80–81 in this chapter for more details on Fair Trade.)

Global Exchange Helps Save Electric Pickup Trucks

In the 1990s, Ford introduced a number of electric vehicles, including pickup trucks, which were 100 percent free of emissions. About 1,500 trucks were produced, most of them going to fleet buyers, and about 200 were leased to individuals. However, in 2004 when Ford decided to abandon electric trucks in favor of hybrid vehicles fueled by a combination of gasoline and batteries, the company asked its leasees to return the electric pickup trucks. The plan was to scrap them.

Global Exchange supported environmentalists who conducted a sit-in for a week at a Ford site in Sacramento, California. In the end, Ford agreed to sell the pickups for $1 to two leaseholders who wanted to keep them and said it was ready to respond to others on a case-by-case basis.

Human Rights Education Associates

Human Rights Education Associates (HREA) was founded in Amsterdam in 1996, and today is located there and in Cambridge, Massachusetts. As one of the newer human rights NGOs, it also depends primarily on the Internet for information and communication. HREA supports learning about human rights, the training of activists and professionals, the development of educational materials and programs, and "community-building through on-line technologies."[80]

HREA issues a number of publications that report on its previous programs or provide background information or other resources to support human rights educators and workers. One of the group's publications is a quarterly online newsletter. The June/July 2004 edition, for example, announced a new ten-week distance-learning course on human rights monitoring. The instructor will be a Bulgarian human rights expert and, because it is online, the students who enroll may be located anywhere.

HREA is working with a number of other groups to support the World Programme for Human Rights Education, announced by the UN Commission on Human Rights. In its first phase, from 2005 to 2007, the groups will focus on promoting learning about human rights in elementary and secondary schools everywhere.[81]

Human Rights First

Human Rights First was founded in New York City in 1978. It was initially known as the Lawyers Committee for Human Rights. Its primary activity is defending for free asylum seekers in the United States and around the world against restrictive immigration laws. Human Rights First also protects human rights activists from persecution by repressive governments and tries to "help build a strong international system of justice and accountability."[82]

Egyptian Human Rights Activist Freed

Saad Ibrahim and two colleagues were imprisoned in Egypt after conducting activities on behalf of human rights in the country. Human Rights First helped mobilize an international campaign on their behalf, assisted in their legal defense, and convinced the United States government to link this case and foreign aid to Egypt. In March 2003, Ibrahim and the others were acquitted and released.

In its 2003 annual report, Human Rights First refers to 12 million people around the world who have left their homeland and are seeking asylum, and up to 25 million who remain in their own country but are displaced as a result of insurgent violence or war.[83] The group also honors human rights heroes at an annual dinner. The 2004 winners were two women who fought for justice against governments that sought to prevent it. Mehrangiz Kar is an Iranian lawyer who was imprisoned for two years before being released and driven to leave the country. Her husband, a journalist, remains in prison. Helen Mack Chang spent ten years trying to get the Guatemalan government to find and punish the murderers of her sister, who was an anthropologist in the country. She received an apology from President Oscar Berger, and several military officers were convicted of the crime. [84]

Human Rights Internet

Human Rights Internet (HRI) is an NGO specializing in exchanging information with international human rights organizations around the world. It was founded in the United States in 1976, but today is located in Ottawa, Canada. HRI's network includes more than 5,000 groups and individuals. HRI has a dual focus. It conducts studies and research in human rights topics and seeks to make them available to governments and NGOs. It also tries to bring technological expertise to human rights NGOs in less developed countries to empower them to fight more effectively against abuses.

One of HRI's weapons is *The Human Rights Tribune*, an online magazine published three times a year. Its motto is "Because

Promoting Human Rights in Iran from the Outside

Mehrangiz Kar is an Iranian lawyer and human rights activist. She was imprisoned in her own country in 2000, tried and convicted, after participating in a symposium in Berlin. Her offense was taking part in a public discussion about Iranian law and politics. She has been a crusader for women's rights in Iran and has dared to state that covering the head is not an intrinsic part of Islam. After serving a six-month sentence, Kar was released and later allowed to travel to Europe for cancer treatments. She is spending the academic year 2004–2005 as a visiting scholar at the Washington College of Law at American University in Washington, D.C.

those who want to change the world know that information is their best defense." According to its website, "The Human Rights Tribune addresses all areas of human rights from a non-governmental perspective. This unique resource can keep you abreast of important developments in the human rights movement world-wide." [85]

On its site, HRI compiles Urgent Alerts from other NGOs. However, unlike Amnesty International, it focuses on continuing situations like the aftermath of the tsunami that hit several countries in Southeast Asia at the end of 2004 rather than the plight of specific individuals.

Getting Children Back to School in Sri Lanka

With more than 200 schools seriously damaged and 32 completely destroyed by the tsunami in late December 2004, school authorities in Sri Lanka have been scrambling to get children back to school. The children's plight is serious, many of them having lost parents or other family members. In this situation, HRI has posted a report from Sri Lanka on its website to help keep the situation at the forefront of international attention.

A Sister's Right to Justice

Helen Mack Chang was a business administrator for a good part of her career in Guatemala until her sister Myrna, a social anthropologist was killed in 1990. From that point, Helen devoted her life to proving that her sister's death was a political crime. After following the case through trials by 12 judges, she saw the soldier who committed the crime sentenced to 30 years in prison. Eventually, the soldier's superiors were also convicted, and Helen Mack Chang received several prizes from human rights organizations for enduring everything from ridicule to death threats in her search for justice for her sister.

Human Strategies for Human Rights

Human Strategies for Human Rights (HSHR) was formed in 2001 and based in Palm Desert, California. Its mission is to combine business management and law to help NGOs do a better job in protecting human rights by working with grassroots groups in many countries. As noted on its website:

> HSHR's approach is that through skills training, the provision of useful information, and the encouragement of conversation circles where local people come together to discuss their problems and to critically think through solutions, that human development, social cohesion, and human rights can be realized.[86]

Peruvian Women Learn about Their Rights

In August 2003, HSHR organized a 6-week workshop for women in Lima, Peru, and some rural neighborhoods outside the capital. Working with Movimento Amplio para Mujeres Linea Fundacional, a local women's network, HSHR provided information about sexual and reproductive rights. In the late 1990s, thousands of poor rural women were sterilized by force by the government. The workshop included an introduction to the concept of human rights and international human rights practices, rights women have in other countries, the international human rights treaties that bind the Peruvian government, and what women can do to safeguard their rights in Peru.

Like Derechos Human Rights, HSHR relies extensively on the advantages of the Internet. Among the services it offers are online mentoring, for example, guiding NGOs in preparing proposals for donors and offering feedback on projects, and answering e-mail questions on points of human rights law and related issues.[87]

Human Rights Watch

Human Rights Watch (HRW) was founded in 1978 as Helsinki Watch. During the Cold War, its mission was to monitor human rights abuses committed by the Soviet Union and its allies that were contrary to the human rights clauses of the 1975 Helsinki Accords. In the 1980s, it set up Americas Watch to focus on Latin America, and the organization grew to cover other regions. In 1988 all the "Watch" committees came together under the umbrella Human Rights Watch. Today it is the largest human rights NGO headquartered in the United States. Its base is in New York City, with offices in Los Angeles, San Francisco, and Washington, D.C. Its European offices are located in Brussels, London, and Moscow, while Asia is covered from Hong Kong.

HRW conducts research and publishes the results in books and reports, "generating extensive coverage in local and international media. This publicity helps to embarrass abusive governments in the eyes of their citizens and the world."[88] For example, in early 2005, HRW targeted Nepal, where King Gyanendra used the Royal Nepalese Army to dismiss the government and declare a state of emergency while imprisoning opponents. HRW also publishes "Monthly Update," an e-mail newsletter that lists the most recent violations of human rights and in some cases adds a "What You Can Do" section, providing an e-mail and/or postal address and phone number for the highest ranking official associated with the abuse. Supporters are urged to make contact and add to the international public outcry against the human rights violation.

International Committee of the Red Cross

The International Committee of the Red Cross includes the International Red Cross and the Red Crescent. Both perform humanitarian work, with Red Crescent focusing on the Muslim world. The International Red Cross was founded in 1863 in Geneva, where it is still headquartered, and "works around the world on a strictly neutral and impartial basis to protect and assist people affected by armed conflicts and internal disturbances."[89]

More than 12,000 staff members are located in permanent offices in 60 countries. The ICRC has operations in more than 80 countries and uses thousands of volunteers as well. Canada and the United States are covered from the office in Washington, D.C. The ICRC also has an office in New York for its permanent delegation to the UN.

One of the chief functions of the ICRC is to monitor and visit prisoners whose cases may involve human rights violations. The prisoners being held by the U.S. military at Guantanamo Bay, Cuba, receive regular visits. The IRC has also visited Abu Ghraib, the prison in Iraq that was the site of human rights abuses by U.S. military personnel. Elsewhere in the Middle East, the ICRC has monitored both sides of the Israeli–Palestinian conflict since 1967. Similarly, it drew international attention to civil rights abuses in Kosovo that helped lead to NATO intervention in the conflict there. ICRC is still responsible for finding missing persons in Kosovo and in other countries of the former Yugoslavia. Many people know the Red Cross primarily for its

Helsinki Accords Focus on Human Rights Abuses in Soviet Empire

The Helsinki Accords of 1975 were the conclusion of the Conference on Security and Cooperation in Europe that lasted for three years. The Accords were signed by the United States, Canada, and every country in Europe with the exception of Albania. Much of the language was devoted to military issues. However, the section on human rights proved to be an effective means of holding the Soviet Union and the six countries in the Warsaw Alliance accountable for violations. Since they signed the Helsinki Accords, their non-compliance with human rights clauses was publicized internationally and kept their governments on the defensive. The continued work of the most famous dissidents like Andrei Sakharov and Lech Walesa led to their receiving the Nobel Peace Prize and—eventually—to their freedom.

work in helping the victims of natural disasters such as hurricanes, floods, and earthquakes. On the international level, however, the ICRC is a major force in protecting individuals and groups at risk during political and genocidal conflicts and wars.

Oxfam International

Oxfam was the original abbreviation for the Oxford Committee for Famine Relief, which was started in England during World War II to provide relief to war victims in Europe. Since then, Oxfam organizations have been established in 12 countries located in Europe, North America, and Australia/Oceania to fight poverty and human rights injustice. In 1995, Oxfam International was created to link them together. One of the leading NGOs in the fight for economic equality, Oxfam considers that "poverty and powerlessness are avoidable and can be eliminated by human action and political will."[90] Using its own employees, consultants, partner organizations, and volunteers, Oxfam aims to empower poor people: "In all our actions our goal is to enable people to exercise their rights and manage their own lives." The organization's approach to fighting poverty and increasing human rights is founded on five aims—"a livelihood; services; security; participation; and diversity."[91]

Oxfam is usually involved in the most visible human and economic rights campaigns and demonstrations. However, this is only part of a policy of combining the specific with the general. "Oxfams link their work on advocacy and campaigning for changes at global and national level to their work on practical changes at grassroots level."[92]

Tsunami Action Links Relief and Trade Policy

In January 2005, Oxfam's home page featured tsunami relief for the refugees but also called for Europe to ease trade regulations so that three of the countries most affected by the December 2004 tsunami—Indonesia,

Maldives, and Sri Lanka—would have a chance to reap more profit from the sales of clothing and shoes, its primary exports. Removing taxes would increase the profit from these countries' exports and thus would help sustain tens of thousands of jobs and generate more foreign exchange. Oxfam pointed out on its website that in 2004 the European Union collected an estimated $75 million from Sri Lanka and $178 million from India in taxes on clothing products—and implied that collecting the same amount in 2005 would exceed the amount of tsunami aid received from the EU. The organization said that by charging these import taxes, the EU is in effect giving with one hand and taking away with the other.

GETTING INVOLVED

As we have seen, most NGOs are concerned with involving people around the world in the fight for human rights. Whether it be to help one political prisoner in a country with an authoritarian regime or to assist a large number of people to acquire land or create fair terms of employment, human rights NGOs need volunteers. Many people join the organizations entirely for humanitarian reasons. Some may be relatives of someone who was deprived of rights or even killed. Others may themselves have been victimized. The majority becomes involved to make a difference and contribute to the expansion of human rights. All of them respond to the idea that the individual matters—which can be the first step toward a grassroots fight for human rights. The first thing that an authoritarian government tries to do is to convince the citizens that only official voices will be heard. Anyone who has an opposing opinion will be dealt with—how severely depends on the degree of repression.

As non-profit organizations, NGOs are always looking for financial contributions from individuals, foundations, and corporations. Some refuse to accept corporate money because they consider big business to be the enemy, but most are ready to collect money from any source other than governments as long as there are no strings attached. On the other hand, NGOs working to promote economic development usually get most of their funding from governments. For example, the United States Agency for International Development (USAID) provides funding for many NGOs in the United States.

NGOs that focus on the defense and spread of human rights around the world often rely primarily on individual contributions. Their websites usually provide a way for individual supporters to make a donation, no matter what the size. However, the biggest contributions are often made by individuals who give of their time and effort rather than their money.

Using Globalization to Promote Fair Trade: TransFair USA

Not everyone agrees on it with Ben Stein that ever-cheaper products are a benefit for producers and consumers. In 1998, an organization called TransFair was founded in Oakland, California, according to "a unique business model that partners industry, farmers, and U.S. consumers to promote equitable trade."*

In its mission statement, TransFair says it wants "to build a more equitable and sustainable model of international trade that benefits producers, consumers, industry, and the earth" It tries to achieve this by labeling products as Fair Trade Certified. Fair Trade certification depends on paying producers of manufactured or agricultural goods "a fair price" that allows farmers to feed their families and send their children to school rather than to work in the fields. TransFair also claims that the fair price means that the producers do not have to "sacrifice quality" in order to keep costs as low as possible. The result is "exceptional products" that are worth the higher price.**

One of the projects that TransFair considers successful involves coffee growers who produce premium coffee beans. In 1999, when the Fair Trade certification of such coffee began, TransFair labeled 2 million pounds of coffee. In 2004, that figure may reach as high as 30 million pounds. That means more farmers and their families are reaping the benfits.

PROJECTS OF THE HEART

"Projects of the Heart" is the title of an article by Tony Vento included in the book *The Global Activist's Manual: Local Ways to Change the World*. He uses "projects of the heart" to describe his success in enlisting Americans of all walks of life to contribute to or at least take an interest in some of the grassroots actions he has been involved in around the world "to put a human face on the global economy."[93] One of his goals has been to interest U.S. citizens in the Fair Trade movement for coffee. It is never easy to convince people to spend more money than they have to, especially for a commodity like coffee.

Vento explains how he does it. He goes to churches and asks people, "What do you think of when you hear *coffee*?" The

However, to put these numbers in perspective, in 2003, the United States imported 2.8 billion pounds of coffee. Although growing, TransFair's impact is not huge. Nevertheless, Paul Rice, TransFair's president, is optimistic. He believes that more and more consumers may be ready to consider ethics when they are shopping. They may want good coffee but they don't like "to feel as if they're contributing to someone's misery."***

TransFair's activities in training coffee growers in marketing and other aspects of contemporary merchandising are possible due to globalization. The expansion of trade around the world has made it profitable for farmers in Latin America and Africa to grow premium coffee beans. To promote its Fair Trade Certification labels, TransFair relies on 21st-century communications, including its website. So far, TransFair USA has worked with coffee, tea, and cocoa producers. In Europe, TransFair has since expanded to include coffee, chocolate, honey, tea, and orange juice.

---

* "Who We Are." Retrieved on July 27, 2004 from *http://www.transfairusa.org/content/about/whoweare.php*.

** "Fair Trade Overview." Retrieved on July 27, 2004 from *http://www.transfairusa.org/content/about/overview.php*.

*** Walker, Rob. "Brewed Awakening? Coffee Beans, Globalization and the Branding of Ethics," *New York Times Magazine*, June 6, 2004, p. 38.

answer always has to do with gourmet coffee and Juan Valdez, the character who promotes Colombian coffee in ads. Then Vento explains that the immaculately dressed, most demanding gentleman has little to do with the harsh realities of picking coffee beans. "Picking coffee in Juan Valdez's outfit would be like wearing a tuxedo to do gardening." He adds that while coffee is something we can choose to do without, for the coffee farmers, it is the difference between life and death. "We ask, what is the reality we're connected to by coffee, and what choices would we want to make?"[94] By simplifying a complex situation to the point where anyone can grasp it, Vento believes he can succeed in getting more Americans involved in his projects. Even if they do not buy Fair Trade-labeled coffee—although he hopes they will—he has still helped Americans clarify their thinking about globalization and perhaps started a process in their development (Figure 6.2). "Once you've shown this is a systemic problem, everyone in the room needs to discover the passion of their heart and dig in on that in a mutual way."[95]

Another example of the difference one person can make is Jeroo Billimoria, a professor of sociology who became horrified by the pitiful condition of abused and abandoned children in her native India (Figure 6.3). During her studies, she had spent two years in New York working with the Coalition for the Homeless. She brought back to India some of the results of those experiences. Having seen the usefulness of free help lines, after three years of lobbying the national Department of Telecommunications, Billimoria succeeded in starting a toll-free telephone help line for Indian children in 1996. Today the 24-hour hotline works in 53 cities and has already assisted more than 3 million children who needed shelter, protection from abuse, medical treatment, counseling, repatriation, and other emergency services.[96]

Although Billimoria was the first executive director of Childline, she stepped down in 2002 in order to move on to further challenges and also to practice what she says she learned

Figure 6.2 These plantation workers are picking coffee beans in Bolombolo, Colombia. By buying Fair Trade coffee the American consumer can support the efforts of coffee workers to improve their quality of life.

Figure 6.3 An Indian baby plays with a comb on a pavement in Calcutta in August 2004. More than 1.2 million destitute, homeless, or orphaned children in India beg on the streets.

from her experience: "to let go." [97] She has gone on to create a new organization, Child Helpline International, creating similar groups in more than 40 countries. [98] Thanks to globalization, Billimoria has moved around the world contributing to improving the lives of the children most at risk. In the next chapter, we look at how the U.S. has responded to globalization and human rights.

America Confronts Globalization and Human Rights

With the end of the Cold War and the breakup of the superpower known as the Soviet Union in the early 1990s, the United States, the world's leading exponent of globalization, remains the only superpower in the early 21st century. Overwhelming military superiority combined with the readiness to use the military allowed the United States and its allies to liberate Kuwait after Iraq invaded the country in 1990. The American military together with allies in NATO bombed Serbia after it committed atrocities of ethnic cleansing in Kosovo in 1999. In 2003, to remove Iraqi leader Saddam Hussein from power and to seize control of weapons of mass destruction allegedly at his disposal, the United States invaded Iraq. All of these actions, the last most of all, were controversial and created enemies for the United States. At the same time, each of them was related to the American desire to

Figure 7.1 A middle-aged couple flees the ruined city of Vukovar, Croatia in the early 1990s. The three-month battle between the Croatian armed forces and the Yugoslavian Federal Army completely destroyed the city and killed thousands of civilians.

guarantee human rights to citizens of a foreign country, in the belief that the methods used were likely to be effective and that the citizens of the foreign country would appreciate and benefit from the American intervention.

In contrast, American diplomats point to what happened when the United States did not take military action. For example, in the early 1990s, thousands died in what is called ethnic cleansing or large-scale genocide in Croatia and Bosnia Herzegovina after Yugoslav President Slobodan Milosevic invaded these parts of the former Yugoslavia to prevent them from becoming independent (Figure 7.1). In 1991, the administration of President George H.W. Bush basically left it to the Europeans to respond to the war in Croatia, and when President Bill Clinton took office in early 1993, his administration followed suit.

Because the European Union responded with words, not bullets, Milosevic continued to deploy his army and paramilitary fighters, extending the war to Bosnia Herzegovina in 1992. The carnage continued for three years, through most of 1995, until the bombing of shoppers at an open-air central food market in Sarajevo mobilized international opinion sufficiently to pressure Milosevic to restore peace by signing the Dayton Peace Accords in December of that year.

Although during this period the UN contributed soldiers and observers, UN soldiers allowed the massacre of 7,000 Bosnian

Sarajevo Marketplace Bombing Leads to Peace

The Balkan wars began in 1991 and ended in late 1995 with the signing of a peace treaty (the Dayton Accords) by Bosnia, Croatia, and Serbia. The wars between Serbia and Croatia, Serbia and Bosnia, and Bosnia and Croatia were wars of independence and wars for territory. Until the early 1990s, all were part of the country called Yugoslavia. At that point, Yugoslavia began to unravel along ethnic lines: Slovenia, Croatia, Macedonia, and Bosnia and Herzegovina were recognized as independent states in 1992. The remaining republics of Serbia and Montenegro declared a new republic of Yugoslavia. In April 1992, Serbia led various military intervention efforts to unite ethnic Serbs in neighboring republics into a "Greater Serbia." It was difficult for Bosnia and Croatia to defend themselves because the rest of the world had declared an arms embargo, leaving only the Serbs—who controlled the former Yugoslav army—with modern armaments.

While Europe and the United States refused to get involved, the killing continued. However, world media coverage focusing on civilian deaths created an atmosphere of outrage that eventually led NATO, spearheaded by the United States, to intervene. The last straw was when Serb soldiers bombed the main marketplace in Sarajevo, capital of Bosnia, twice, firing on the city from surrounding mountains. The first bombing in February 1994 cost 68 lives. The second, in August 1995, killed 37 shoppers; two days later, NATO planes bombed Serbian forces in Bosnia and forced their retreat from the outskirts of Sarajevo.

men and boys in the so-called safe haven of Srebrenica less than two months before the signing of the Dayton Accords. It took the muscle of American and other NATO troops who replaced UN troops in Croatia and Bosnia at the end of 1995 to stop bloodshed in the country. Some troops are still there and making slow progress in securing and expanding human rights for all ethnic groups.

GLOBALIZATION AND SEPTEMBER 11, 2001

Even for a superpower, military superiority does not guarantee safety. The United States suffered the most casualties ever inflicted on its own soil on September 11, 2001, when armed hijackers took over four passenger jets and rammed two of them into the World Trade Center towers in New York and one into the Pentagon building in Washington, D.C. The fourth jet crashed in rural Pennsylvania, probably on its way to another target in the nation's capital, after a revolt by the passengers brought the plane down. That day showed Americans that they were not safe on their own territory—regardless of how many weapons and troops they might have. In addition to everything else it signified, September 11 proved to Americans and the world that globalization could provide technology and communications to a small group of men fanatically committed to a cause and facilitate their killing 3,000 people in the heart of the reigning superpower (Figure 7.2).

Writer Thomas Friedman has identified two basic responses to globalization. One is to use the power of the Internet and high technology to leap frontiers and oceans to create new centers of business. This has happened in India, he says, where the call center and software companies are good enough to compete for clients with the best in the world and often win. This is the response that reflects and increases personal freedom. Young Indians attend schools and universities where they receive excellent training in technology and bring to their jobs the motivation to live better and differently than their parents.

Figure 7.2 The South Tower of the World Trade Center explodes into flames after being struck by a hijacked airliner. The fact that some around the world rejoiced at the disaster came as a shock to many Americans, but to others it was the moment they realized that they, like the rest of the world, were vulnerable to terrorist attacks.

As we saw in Chapters 1 and 3, their lives are full of increased possibilities and they look ahead to an exciting future.

The other response to globalization is the route taken by fundamentalist extremists. Their brand of religion begins by denying human rights to women. In many cases girls are banned from school entirely or permitted only a few grades of elementary schooling and are prevented from receiving the education or training given to their brothers. The countries where this type of fundamentalist religion is taught—Pakistan, Saudi Arabia, and Afghanistan under the Taliban—are autocratic societies where religious authorities terrorize the population, "societies where there was no democracy and where fundamentalists have often suffocated women and intellectuals who crave science, free thinking and rationality."[99]

The brothers of the girls whose schooling is limited attend schools for boys only called *madrassas* where they are taught according to an extremist interpretation of the Koran.[100] Later, mainly in Western countries, they are educated in technology and state-of-the-art communications, but they do not use that knowledge to expand their own horizons and improve the lives of their fellow citizens. They use it only for destruction, of themselves and as many others as they can kill. Their primary targets are Americans, but, as in the World Trade Center, where more than 3,000 people including many Muslims from 13 other countries died, and the bombings in Madrid and Bali, the goal is to wreak havoc and kill because they cannot imagine a better future on earth.

IT ISN'T EASY BEING A SUPERPOWER

On September 11, 2001 people in many countries rejoiced at the blow dealt to the United States, shocking Americans who prefer to believe they are universally liked. However, that was the reaction of a few. Most of the world mourned along with America. The hard fact for Americans to accept is that because the United States throws its military weight around and because it is the richest country, it has a hard time being liked. Some accuse the United States of being a bully. Others claim it does not pay a fair share of the cost of the United Nations or give enough aid to economically troubled nations. The United States is also faulted for preaching human rights while being far less than perfect in honoring them inside and outside the country. However, the biggest problem the United States faces in the world is the pervasiveness of its culture, which many proclaim to be flawed, while an equal or greater number want to copy it.

In considering the situation of the United States compared to other superpowers in their day, such as Britain in the 19th century, Rome in the Roman Empire, or China at various times, Zbigniew Brzezinski finds that "[u]nlike previous . . . powers, America operates in a world of intensifying immediacy and intimacy." The earlier superpowers were insulated by their borders and "relatively impervious to external threats." The United States today is not. Despite America's military might, "its homeland is uniquely insecure." The only solution Brzezinski sees is for the United States to understand and accept that globalization "means global interdependence." This implies that no one, not even the superpower,

> has total immunity from the consequences of the technological revolution that has so vastly increased the human capability to inflict violence and yet tightened the bonds that increasingly tie humanity together.[101]

For Brzezinski, globalization has brought America to the point of being "the catalyst either for a global community or for global chaos . . . . Our choice is between dominating the world and leading it."[102]

LEADING THE WORLD CREATES ENVY AND RESENTMENT

Thomas Friedman believes America is leading the world, but the world often resists being led into globalization. Those who oppose both America and globalization feel "envy and resentment toward the United States—envy because America seems so much better at riding this tiger, and resentment because Americanization–globalization so often feels like the United States whipping everyone to speed up." He goes on to quote the historian Ronald Steel, who once called the United States a "revolutionary power" as opposed to the Soviet Union.[103] Although the Soviet Union was founded through a genuine revolution and claimed to stand for perpetual betterment of humanity, it proved to be conservative and fatally immobile in the end. Brzezinski makes a similar point in discussing how America has been and continues to be a destabilizing force in much of the world by its support for democracy and the pervasiveness of its culture.[104]

People all over the world have come to know and believe they understand American culture, meaning they are familiar with Hollywood films, popular music, some books, and international logos and products like McDonalds, Nike, Levi Strauss, Kodak, Dell, and Ford. They have seen New York, Los Angeles, and Chicago in movies or videos, and feel they know those cities. Because of this exposure, they believe they understand America with a confidence that Americans never feel when faced with the culture of another country.

That apparent familiarity has important consequences for how much of the world reacts to the United States Brzezinski cites international polls implying "that virtual familiarity breeds affection for much of the American way of life even as it intensifies resentment of U.S. policies."[105] People embrace the American lifestyle or those aspects like popular branded products available to them at the same time that they strongly criticize America's role in the world. Brzezinski thinks this may be "the major political consequence of America's cultural seduction." He suggests that it is a

double-edged compliment by those who truly expect more from America and resent its failure to meet such elevated expectations when it comes to actual policy. Anti-Americanism bears the trappings of betrayed affection.[106]

AMERICAN ECONOMIC LEADERSHIP

The U.S. leadership in globalization is expressed first of all through its commitment to free trade and open markets. While that commitment sometimes gets side-tracked by special interests who lobby for higher steel prices, a guaranteed price for sugar or citrus, or some other form of protection and special treatment, it is, nonetheless, America that provides the primary funding and support for the chief institutions monitoring and managing world economic development: the World Bank, the International Monetary Fund, and the World Trade Organization. Indeed, the first two are headquartered in Washington, D.C., though they have offices in other countries as well.

Because Americans dislike ideology and prefer the practical, globalization which—as Brzezinski says—seems to be objective is now "the informal ideology of the U.S. political and business elite, defining America's role in the world." In a number of speeches cited by Brzezinski, former President Bill Clinton repeated his belief in "the historical inevitability, social desirability, and need for American political leadership of mankind's march into the era of globalization." In this remark, Clinton strongly links globalization and democracy and, by extension, human rights:

> Those who believe globalization is only about market economies, however, are wrong too . . . . We must recognize first that globalization has made us all more free and more interdependent.[107]

LINKING TRADE AND HUMAN RIGHTS

The demonstrations launched by some NGOs against the World Bank—in Washington, D.C. in April 2000 and in Prague in September 2000 and the World Trade Organization in Seattle in December 1999—in recent years were intended to increase the linkage between trade benefits and human rights guarantees, especially relating to labor. According to this view, it is not enough to lower barriers and create freer trade among nations; the economic power of stronger and richer countries must be used to force weaker and poorer countries to adopt standards such as the International Labour Organization's requirements. Protestors believe that issues such as the right to organize in unions, the right to strike, the right to a living wage, and the abolition of child labor should be guaranteed in trade agreements and economic development loans and in programs brokered by international organizations (Figure 7.3). This has been referred to as the Social Clause, and it is what some have tried to incorporate into the World Trade Organization's operating regulations.

Responding to lobbying by trade unions, some developed countries, in general those with a tendency to support greater socialism, have generally agreed with the demand to link freer trade with labor requirements. But many less developed and poorer countries have opposed the Social Clause. Their weaker economies could not afford the pay scales and other rights of organized labor that predominate in the wealthier countries. The current solution to this problem is to include in trade agreements something that obligates each country to observe its own labor laws. The U.S. Congress has tended to go in this direction in trade agreements with other countries. It has also written this kind of language into the so-called fast-track legislation that allows the U.S. President to negotiate trade deals and present them to Congress for a simple yes or no vote. Under fast-track, Congress may not add or subtract amendments to the proposed legislation.[108]

Jagdish Bhagwati objects, however, to writing labor requirements into trading agreements. He says that it is a foot in the door for unions, allowing them to go on to raise demands; in the case of the Central American free trade agreements, countries are being asked to raise their labor standards, not just maintain them. He insists that each country must be free to set its labor standards according to its own needs. "Restrictions on the flexibility of standards setting, even if hedged by safeguards, are not

Figure 7.3 Protestors held police at bay near the convention center during the World Trade Organization trade talks in Seattle in December 1999. Tens of thousands of people filled the downtown area, blocking traffic and chanting. The American public was shocked by the violence they saw and the events grabbed the world's attention. Protests such as this one have accompanied the meetings of the World Trade Organization at other locations around the world.

a good idea compared to dialogue and persuasion . . . ." Finally, many laws, especially in poor countries, "have been enacted without any intention to implement them." [109] For all these reasons, he believes it is better to omit the strict requirements in trade agreements at all levels and instead focus on the impact of a public airing. Citing NGOs and CNN for their ability to broadcast worldwide by Internet and satellite television, respectively, Bhagwati concludes,

> we have the possibility now of using shame and embarrassment to great advantage . . . . These techniques can unleash . . . the Dracula effect: expose evil to sunlight and it will shrivel up and die.[110]

JUDICIAL ACTIVISM, AMERICA, AND GLOBAL HUMAN RIGHTS

Another way that globalization may help protect human rights in the future—at least in wealthier countries—is as the result of international judicial activism. Bhagwati calls this a "new trend," whose beginnings he finds in the Bangalore Principles of Judicial Conduct that came out of a symposium of legal experts held in 1988 in Bangalore, India. The Bangalore Principles call for judicial independence and integrity to assure equal treatment under the law for plaintiffs in all countries. Ruth Bader Ginsburg, who today sits on the U.S. Supreme Court, was one of the jurists who participated. The participants issued a statement "that expounded principles that have had a huge impact on judicial thinking worldwide." According to Bhagwati, in the statement,

> They cited and approved the "growing tendency for national courts to have regard to [evolving] international norms for the purpose of deciding cases where the domestic law—whether constitutional, statute or common law—is uncertain or incomplete."[111]

On the other hand, Bhagwati strongly criticizes what has happened in American courts, where since 1980 Americans have sued non-Americans for alleged human rights violations that took place in other countries. The lawyers who try such cases rely on the 1789 Alien Torts Act. Regardless of the merits of any specific case, he considers this the wrong kind of judicial activism, since

U.S. courts are giving themselves universal jurisdiction that other countries do not recognize. Calling it "judicial imperialism," he notes that many foreigners consider this behavior "to reflect the moral arrogance and hubris that Americans are far too often accused of."

Foreign Leaders Sued in U.S. Courts

In 2000, the former Chinese Prime Minister Li Peng was sued in an American court for his role in cracking down on Chinese students during the Tiananmen Square massacre in Beijing in 1989. His accusers were five natives of China. Thus, a serious allegation of human rights abuses that took place in another country, directed by a foreigner, and with foreigners as victims, was nonetheless tried in a court in the United States.

Would Americans like to see Americans suing each other in foreign courts over matters that took place in the United States?[112] It must be added too that many Americans do not favor allowing international courts to influence legal decisions in U.S. courts. This is one of the many areas where being for or against globalization depends on the specific case.

THE UNITED STATES, HUMAN RIGHTS, AND GLOBALIZATION AFTER SEPTEMBER 11

Congress established the U.S. Institute of Peace (USIP) in 1984 as an independent non-partisan federal agency "to promote the prevention, management, and peaceful resolution of international conflicts."[113] USIP conducts research and works in countries at risk because of chaos in the aftermath of war. For example, it is active today in Afghanistan and Iraq. Just after September 11, 2001, the Institute sponsored a symposium on how to balance "the United States's traditional commitment to advancing human rights and democracy" and "the new order created by the war on terrorism."[114]

Participants included current and former government officials. Each speaker affirmed that America had to continue to urge the expansion of human rights, and some emphasized that in the atmosphere following September 11, extending human rights in countries where they were seldom observed was more important than ever. Elliott Abrams, the National Security Council staff chief for Democracy, Human Rights, and International Operations, explained that the Bush administration had to determine "how to encourage rule of law and respect for human rights in numerous countries in the Islamic world where neither of these matters are in very good shape." He went on to say that people in that part of the world "often believe that they must choose between secular tyranny and religious tyranny." The United States must help people understand that there is a third way.[115]

Assistant Secretary of State Lorne Craner looked back at recent history and said that during the 1980s, U.S. human rights policy abroad focused on elections. In the 1990s, the emphasis was on building institutions of civil society, NGOs, chambers of commerce, and other private organizations not beholden to any government. In the first decade of the 21st century, the focus will be on assistance to "new democratic rulers" to help them "govern in a manner that advances democratic practices and economic well-being while also ending corruption."[116]

Professor John Norton Moore of the University of Virginia reminded the group that on September 11, 2001, the United States "was not attacked for doing something wrong." He rejected the various reasons mentioned by Osama bin Laden in messages and interviews, especially the claim that America is anti-Islam, and noted that the last three wars the United States fought—in Kuwait, Kosovo, and Bosnia—"were all fought to protect Muslims." Instead, America "was attacked because of the ideals it represents on human freedom and democracy." Moore concluded that where democracy and human rights are absent, war, terrorism, corruption, and refugees are often the result.[117] In the next chapter, we consider the future of human rights under globalization.

The Future of Human Rights Under Globalization

Few who are not extremists or fundamentalists believe that globalization can or even should be rolled back. For better or worse, once exposed to the Internet and jet travel, few would consider living in a world without instant communications and easy transportation. In the same way, few involved in international trade as producers or consumers are agitating to replace it with the restricted local and national markets of the past. Most of the discussion of globalization today has to do with how to manage, steer, and upgrade globalization so that it brings the greatest benefit to the greatest number of people and spreads the benefits more evenly around the world, leaving no country or region behind.

Intertwined in that discussion of globalization is the role of human rights. Up to now, globalization has not always led to an increase of human rights, according to its opponents. They argue that free trade sometimes collapses the economic rights of one group of people in reducing the value of their work, leaving them without a living wage or any wage at all if their jobs disappear. In other cases, critics of globalization find that while one set of people may benefit as a result of free trade, another is victimized as their rights are reduced or taken away.

GLOBALIZATION AND THE FUTURE OF WOMEN'S RIGHTS

In the United Nations Fourth World Conference on Women, held in Beijing in 1995, women's rights were brought "more explicitly into the mainstream of international human rights discussions (Figure 8.1)."[118] In the Beijing Declaration that was issued at the end of the conference, the delegates "reaffirm[ed] their] commitment to . . . [e]nsure the full implementation of the human rights of women and of the girl child as an inalienable, integral, and indivisible part of all human rights and fundamental freedoms."[119]

In the action sections of the document, the delegates stated that they were determined to:

> Intensify efforts to ensure equal enjoyment of all human rights and fundamental freedoms for all women and girls who face multiple barriers to their empowerment and advancement because of such factors as their race, language, ethnicity, culture, religion, or disability, or because they are indigenous people.[120]

The final action section of the Beijing Declaration seeks to guarantee "access to economic resources including land, credit, science and technology, vocational training, information, communication and markets" in order to enable "the advancement and empowerment of women and girls . . . ."[121]

The Beijing Declaration gave supporters of women's rights another weapon in the international fight against abuses and violations. However, even experts like Jagdish Bhagwati, who

Figure 8.1 An inflatable dove floats above the attendees at a welcome ceremony for delegates to the UN World Conference on Women held in Beijing's Great Hall of the People on Monday, September 4, 1995.

generally defend globalization, admit that so far it has not always been kind or fair to women. He uses as one example the problems that women who take positions as servants encounter in countries like Saudi Arabia "where local women are typically living in the Middle Ages and under Islamic laws as interpreted by illiterate and conservative religious leaders."[122] As another example, female servants from countries like Russia, Philippines, and Malaysia that export labor are sometimes treated like slaves by their foreign employers. Many of these women are victims of economic restructuring or financial crises that result from their own countries' attempts to keep up with globalization. The Philippines and Malaysia are both sites for inexpensive production of goods shipped around the world. As production depends more on technology and less on humn labor, thousands of people emigrate from these countries to find work.

While tourism is a generally positive aspect of globalization, increasing incomes in developing countries popular with foreign visitors, it also has harmed women in countries such as Thailand, where cheap prostitution is one of the attractions being offered along with perfect beaches and fresh seafood. Whether employed as sex workers or as servants, many of these women are treated as commodities by criminals who create industries out of their exploitation.[123] Unfortunately, as Alison Brysk has noted, police and other authorities are often involved in such illegal industries and hardly interested in protecting the women.[124]

If every country closed its borders to foreign tourists and workers, such abuses could be halted. But would it be possible and would it be better to confine people within their national borders? Freedom of movement is also an important human right that affects women and men. Learning about other countries as a tourist or an employee is also desirable. The more people know about other countries, the less likelihood there is of conflicts coming from misunderstanding.

The kinds of abuses of women related to globalization could easily be alleviated at the national level both by the countries that supply the women and those that import them. Better enforcement of laws against criminal trafficking and more protection for human rights of women in every country would go a long way toward solving the worst problems. Moreover, lifting regulations that are stifling a country's economy can open it for both foreign and domestic investment, creating jobs and raising the standard of living. In a period of national economic expansion, women do better, feeling less need to emigrate to find work and enjoying more civilized conditions abroad if they do.

GLOBALIZATION AND THE FUTURE OF CHILD LABOR

Jagdish Bhagwati emphatically insists that abuses of child labor are unrelated to globalization. He tells the story of a child working as a servant in an Indian household who was beaten and burned by his employer for drinking some milk not finished by the man's children. This incident was used by an NGO to attack globalization. Bhagwati concludes as any sensible person would that the situation—awful as it was—was caused by an evil person and not an evil international economic system.[125]

According to Bhagwati, three recent studies have shown that as soon as poor parents have more money or the ability to borrow money, they use some of it to send their children to school. It is only the very poor with no prospects of changing their economic condition who make their children work—and they do so as a last resort. When a country's economy gets worse and credit gets tight, people take their children out of school and send them to work in the fields or in sweatshops.[126]

Child labor is not always the worst scenario in a developing country. Bhagwati believes that in the case of a poor country, it is wrong for domestic or international legislation to mandate an end to child labor. In 1993, clothing factories in Bangladesh kicked out some 50,000 child workers because they expected that the U.S. Child Labor Deterrence Act would be passed. As a result, some of the young girls who lost their jobs went to work in the underground economy or even became prostitutes.[127]

Legrain cites a study—mentioned in Chapter 3—that showed that in the poorest countries with annual income per person of less than $500 per year, 30 to 60 percent of children aged 10 to 14 work. In countries with an annual income of $500 to $1,000 per year, the numbers of children aged 10 to 14 working drop to 10 to 30 percent.[128]

As with human rights abuses against women, if child labor is to be controlled, it must be done by local legislation that provides severe punishment for abusers like the Indian employer in Bhagwati's example. Both Bhagwati and Legrain agree that child labor declines as incomes rise and opportunities expand. Child labor will decrease and eventually disappear as a country becomes richer because most parents want their children to get an education. The more available jobs and the clearer the relationship between jobs and education, the better both generations will do.

GLOBALIZATION AND LABOR ABUSES

Some critics of globalization have claimed for years that multinational companies from rich countries employ subcontractors in less developed countries who mistreat their employees, paying them less than a living wage or providing inadequate working conditions. In 1995, the entertainer Kathie Lee Gifford was involved in an embarrassing situation when it was found that clothes sold under her label were manufactured in sweatshops in Honduras. As exposed by the National Labor Committee, an American NGO, women employees, including 13-year-old girls, were working up to 75 hours per week and treated in a humiliating manner by male armed guards.

Gifford and her husband, Frank Gifford, became personally involved in overseeing the improvement of the factory and the eventual restoration of its contract with Wal-Mart, the company for whom the Kathie Lee Gifford label clothes were being produced. Eventually workers were paid everything due to them.[129]

Two years later, sweatshop conditions were found in two small New York City factories employing Chinese immigrant women. These factories also produced clothes sold under the Kathie Lee Gifford label for Wal-Mart, Kmart, Nordstrom, and Lerner shops, a subsidiary of The Limited. Although the New York factories were unionized, the owner kept double books and didn't pay the Chinese employees all the money that was due to them. The U.S. Labor Department discovered the crime, imposed heavy fines on the owner, and made the owner pay back wages to employees.[130]

In 2004, the clothing maker Gap Inc. admitted to labor violations among some of its contract manufacturers outside the United States. Issuing its first "social responsibility" report at the 2004 annual shareholders' meeting, Gap said it had found thousands of examples of mistreatment of workers among its 3,009 factories in 50 countries. The most violations were found in Gap's 241 factories in China, 73 of which "received the company's two lowest grades—'needs improvement' or 'immediate attention required.'"[131]

To create the report, the company sent 90 investigators around the world to evaluate conditions at its contract manufacturers that possibly employ—according to one estimate—as many as 300,000 workers. Companies cited in the report were told to fix the violations, according to Gap's chief administrative and compliance officer. "If a factory repeatedly violates the rules, Gap said it dumps the offending manufacturer." In 2003, Gap fired 136 factories, 84 of them in China and Southeast Asia.[132]

In these cases, labor violations abroad came to the attention of an NGO and were investigated by a major multinational company. Those in the United States were eventually identified by the U.S. government and punished accordingly. Exposure of the situation, holding individuals and companies accountable, and focusing mass media publicity on everything helped to solve problems. This seems to be the best way to deal with human rights abuses in labor, as it is in other areas. As Legrain says, it is up to developing countries and developed ones, too, to respond to local pressure and "to enforce labour laws that suit their local conditions."[133]

FIGHTING TORTURE THROUGH GLOBALIZATION

On January 1, 1988, the UN Committee against Torture began operations as a result of Article 17 of the Convention against Torture and Other Cruel, Inhuman, or Degrading Treatment or Punishment, which came into effect in mid-1987. Consisting of ten members from ten countries elected by UN member nations that have ratified the Convention, the Committee hears reports from countries and individuals and is empowered to conduct investigations into allegations of torture.[134] Like other human rights organizations under the United Nations umbrella, it employs a special reporter or rapporteur who collects information and personally visits victims of alleged torture prior to preparing a report evaluating the situation.

Torture is a technique officially, and sometimes unofficially or illegally, employed by many nations around the world as a means of forcing information out of an unwilling person. In most democracies the discovery of the use of torture results in severe punishment of the perpetrator or groups involved. It may be used in situations where individuals take it upon themselves to settle scores or impart punishment on their own. This may be what happened at the Abu Ghraib prison outside Baghdad, when at least some Iraqi prisoners were subjected to cruel and inhumane treatment at the hands of their U.S. captors—although in most cases their lives were not at risk.

Although it may be a normal procedure for creating fear and enforcing power in some situations, no democratic governments and few governments in general admit to using torture. International exposure through mass media, universal disapproval, and sanctions in cases where torture is not an exception but an accepted policy seem to be the best way to combat torture in countries where citizens do not have the right to express their opinions about torture and to vote governments that perpetuate it out of office. In democracies, allegations of torture will often lead to media investigation and legal action by the victims while official channels are used to punish the perpetrators. This is what is happening with those accused of torture in the Abu Ghraib situation.

A NEW ROLE FOR GLOBAL BUSINESS IN EXTENDING HUMAN RIGHTS

John Kamm is the founder and chairman of the Dui Hua Foundation, which is based in San Francisco. He was a regional vice-president for Occidental Petroleum Corporation and president of the American Chamber of Commerce in Hong Kong. He has extensive experience doing business with China and used the Chinese word for dialogue as the name of his foundation when he established it in 1999.

In 1990, one year after the Tiananmen Square massacre in Beijing suppressed pro-democracy student demonstrations, Kamm was heading to Washington, D.C., to testify before Congress in favor of granting China favorable trading status despite its violations of human rights. In June 1989, the Chinese government had used tanks to clear Tiananmen Square of young demonstrators. The number of young people killed is still being debated, but there were some deaths and many more people were imprisoned. Kamm knew that Congress would seize on these human rights violations as a reason to deny Most Favored Nation (MFN) trading status and thought that would be a mistake.

Making the toast at a luncheon given by Beijing's senior representative in Hong Kong to thank the American business people at the American Chamber of Commerce for supporting China's application for MFN, Kamm suddenly asked the Chinese diplomat, "Why don't you free Yao Yongzhan?" Yao was a young student from Hong Kong whom the Chinese had recently arrested in Shanghai and were allegedly torturing.

The Chinese diplomat was outraged. Other members of the American Chamber apologized for Kamm's question. However, Kamm noticed that one month later, Yao was released from prison.[135] That experience led to Kamm's resignation from his job at Occidental and the eventual establishment of Dui Hua, a foundation that collects information about prisoners being held in China in violation of their human rights. Based on his success with freeing the Hong Kong student, Kamm visits Hong Kong and other parts of China regularly, bringing lists of prisoners and asking for their release (Figure 8.2). In 2002, Kamm believed he has been at least partly responsible for about 250 prisoners being released or given better treatment in prison. No other person or organization in the world, including the State Department, has helped more Chinese prisoners.[136]

Yao Yongzhan Continues Dissident Activities outside China

Yao Yongzhan, like many of the student leaders from Tiananmen Square demonstration and massacre, has been living in exile for several years. He continues to work for greater freedom and democracy in China. On the 15th anniversary of the Tiananmen Square movement and its suppression on June 4, 2004, Yao and several others conducted a hunger strike in front of the Chinese Embassy in Washington, D.C.

Kamm believes that human rights activities need not be left only to governments and activists:

Business people can also take many simple steps to promote a better general environment for the respect of human rights. They can monitor human rights conditions where they operate and provide that information to non-governmental organizations. They can lobby governments to make systemic reforms to strengthen human rights . . . . Outsiders will not be the driving force for change in a country. The people of that nation will fill that role. However, outsiders can assist by helping those agents for change get out of prison so they can do their work. The basis of the free enterprise system is individuals making free choices. If individuals cannot make free choices, the free enterprise system does not work.[137]

Figure 8.2 Tibetan nun Ngawang Sangdrol was being held in a prison in China for participating in pro-independence protests. She was first arrested in 1990 at the age of 13. She was not due to be released until 2013, but through the efforts of John Kamm and others she was freed on a medical parole in October 2002. She has continued to work on human rights issues since her release.

He explained his interest in promoting human rights in China as follows: "To say trade is good for human rights is to put the cart before the horse. It is human rights that are good for business."[138]

A similar approach is taken by BSR, or Business for Social Responsibility, an organization established in 1992 by a group of 50 companies "dedicated to helping businesses be both commercially successful and socially responsible."[139] BSR believes that "market and social forces are creating pressure to focus on the company's impact on human rights anywhere in the world business is conducted."[140]

Kamm and BSR promote codes of conduct for business that incorporate human rights because they believe the codes are not only the right thing to do but also the most effective way for business to behave in the globalized world. There is every reason to expect that more and more companies will concern themselves with the impact of their activities and policies on human rights in the countries where they operate because international consumers and stakeholders will demand it.

GLOBAL HUMAN RIGHTS DEPEND ON GOOD GOVERNANCE

Critics and supporters of globalization tend to agree that what is needed worldwide is good governance at many levels. The word *governance* refers to how international organizations like the United Nations, the World Bank, and the World Trade Organization construct their operations so as to have the maximum impact on human rights. Good governance refers also to the effectiveness of national governments in guaranteeing human rights and protecting their citizens from abuses and violations.

Author Thomas Friedman compares the response of the Indian and Chinese governments to the increased globalization of their economies. He draws a distinction between what he calls the hardware and the software of democracy. The hardware of democracy is free elections, and India has those. The software of democracy includes "decent, responsive, transparent local government," which India does not have. Although China has no hardware "in the form of free elections, its institutions have been better at building infrastructure and services for China's people and foreign investors." So, unlike India, China has the software of infrastructure and service that may lead in time to political democracy. But, says Friedman, it is best to have both. It is not possible for a modern high-technology industry to develop, according to Friedman,

> when every company has to build its own infrastructure. American's greatest competitive advantages are the flexibility of its economy and the quality of its infrastructure, rule of law and regulatory institutions.[141]

The national elections in India in April and May 2004 threw out the ruling Bharatiya Janata Party and returned the Congress Party to power. The Congress Party which was established in 1885 while India was still part of Britain's colonial empire has been the leading party in India ever since the country became independent in 1947. The Bharatiya Janata Party which was established in 1925 came to lead India in the 1990s. Under its leadership, India began to make strides in economic globalization, but it was defeated at the polls in 2004. Although some from the antiglobalization camp said that the election results represented a rejection of globalization, Friedman disagrees. "The Indian masses didn't vote for an antiglobalization strategy, they voted for (among other things) an *effective* globalization strategy." India's new prime minister Manmohan Singh has the "task now to make globalization work for more Indians by making the government work for more Indians."[142] The World Bank and the World Trade Organization also have begun to pay attention to good governance issues as they concern themselves more with the human rights impact of their economic decisions.

THE FUTURE OF HUMAN RIGHTS IN A GLOBALIZED WORLD

It will be more and more difficult for any country to make decisions that have a negative effect on the human rights of its own citizens or foreigners without running into an international media storm generated by NGOs, mass media, and democratic countries, often led by the United States. Although, as Alison Brysk has noted, media does not reach all segments of society in many countries, nonetheless the prospect is that mass communications are becoming ever cheaper and more widely available. [143] She too agrees that mass communications make it possible for information to bypass the barriers put up by authoritarian governments. [144]

However, much still depends on the goodwill and initiative of individual countries, because many people identify much more with their own country than with any international body like the United Nations or the European Union. In a review of *How Soccer Explains the World: An Unlikely Theory of Globalization*, Edward Rothstein notes that "[r]eports of the death of nationalism are, apparently, highly exaggerated." [145]

While it is true that there is international trade in players, and that Polish soccer stars play in Madrid and Dutch stars in Manchester, most fans are loyal to the death to their national team. This is hard for Americans, who have so many kinds of sports and so many local teams to cheer for, to understand. National teams in the United States are found only in basketball, hockey, and soccer in the Olympics, and they seldom enjoy the attention accorded to the most glamorous local teams like the Dallas Cowboys, the New York Yankees, and the Los Angeles Lakers. But Rothstein's point is that for all the talk, globalization is still rather vague to many and does not stir people's hearts the way rooting for a specific team can do. It is an interesting counterpoint to the general fascination with globalization.

Many Americans are at heart still isolationist. They prefer to pay attention to the rest of the world only when it intrudes into American consciousness and daily life. Donnelly finds, "many

Americans are reluctant to spend money or risk American lives to support human rights abroad."[146] On the other hand, as the events of September 11 and the war in Iraq show, it is hard for America to remain isolationist, especially in the new age of globalized terrorism.

A final word about how much a superpower can accomplish and what it cannot do comes from a man who has seen both sides. While most people recognize that massive military solutions are the only ones that work in extreme situations, they also realize that military solutions are not always the most effective. To provide humanitarian assistance when there is armed conflict or after a natural disaster, more modest approaches may be more effective.

Jan Egeland of Norway is the United Nations' Under-Secretary-General for Humanitarian Affairs and Emergency Relief Coordinator. In the 1980s he wrote *Impotent Superpower—Potent Small State*, a book in which he argued that Norway, a small country, is the world leader in contributing to economic development because it reserves a higher percentage of its national wealth for aid than any other country, large or small. He claimed that "in human rights, the effectiveness of a superpower is overrated and the potential of the small state is underrated." Egeland adds that today,

> Norway is very quick and bold and entrepreneurial in international work, and that is why it is playing such a role in conflict areas and in so much humanitarian work.

However, he says if he were writing that book in 2004, he would acknowledge "that the superpower is totally needed for things to work." Without the European Union or the United States "we're just lost."[147] Egeland recognizes that small countries have only limited power and funds in most situations and international organizations—including the UN where he works—often cannot move fast enough to save people facing natural or man-made disaster.

HUMAN RIGHTS ORGANIZATIONS

NGOs

Amnesty International *http://web.amnesty.org*
Worldwide, founded in 1961, with over 1.8 million members in 150 countries. Awarded the Nobel Peace Prize in 1977 for assisting political prisoners and fighting torture.

Derechos Human Rights *www.derechos.org*
Worldwide but focused on Latin America, first Internet-based human rights NGO.

Freedom House *http://www.freedomhouse.org*
Founded in 1941 and oldest American human rights NGO. Each year it produces the *Freedom in the World* survey rating countries on civil liberties and political rights.

Global Exchange *http://www.globalexchange.org/about/index.html*
Founded in San Francisco in 1988 to focus on economic issues affecting international relations.

Human Rights Education Associates *www.hrea.org*
Founded in Amsterdam in 1996, located there and in Cambridge, Massachusetts, to train people in the Third World in human rights and how to fight for them.

Human Rights First *www.humanrightsfirst.org*
Started in 1978 as the Lawyers Committee for Human Rights and known as Human Rights First since 2004. It defends asylum seekers in the United States and around the world against restrictive immigration laws.

Human Rights Internet *http://www.hri.ca/about/intro.shtml*
Founded in the United States in 1976, now located in Ottawa, Canada. It exchanges information with international human rights organizations around the world.

Human Strategy for Human Rights *www.hshr.org*
Formed in 2001 and based in Palm Desert, California. It combines business, management, and law in working with grassroots groups in many countries.

Human Rights Watch *http://www.hrw.org*
Began in 1978 as Helsinki Watch to monitor human rights abuses by the Soviet Union and its allies. Now it covers the world from New York and other offices around the world.

The International Committee of the Red Cross *http://www.icrc.org/eng*
Founded in 1863 in Geneva, Switzerland, as the Red Cross, today its 12,000 staff members are with the International Red Cross and the Red Crescent performing humanitarian work, with Red Crescent focusing on the Muslim world.

Oxfam International *www.oxfam.org*
Founded in 1995 to link 12 organizations in Europe, Canada, United States, and Asia-Pacific to fight poverty and human rights injustice in more than 100 countries.

NONPROFIT ORGANIZATIONS

Business for Social Responsibility *www.bsr.org*
Founded in 1992 to help companies achieve success through ethical practices. It is a global group that promotes support for human rights as part of the cost of doing business.

The Dui Hua Foundation *www.duihua.org*
Founded in 1997 in San Francisco to work for human rights by contributing to the dialogue between the United States and China.

TransFair USA *www.transfairusa.org*
Since 1999, TransFair has certified Fair Trade prices for commodities like coffee and tried to guarantee international prices that allow farmers in poor countries a decent standard of living.

U.S. Institute of Peace *www.usip.org*
Established in 1984 by the Congress of the United States as an independent organization to assist in resolving international conflicts. It is active wherever human rights are threatened during military action.

UNITED NATIONS AGENCIES

Commission on Human Rights *http://www.ohchr.org/english/bodies/chr/index.htm*
Established in 1946, today has 53 member countries that meet for six weeks every spring in Geneva to go over human rights issues. More than 3,000 delegates from member and observer countries as well as NGOs attend. The 2005 session was held from March 14 to April 22.

Human Rights Committee *www.ohchr.org/english/bodies/hrc/index.htm*
Works out of the Office of the High Commissioner for Human Rights and manages a group of independent experts who testify about human rights violations.

International Labour Organization *www.ilo.org*
Founded in 1919 by the League of Nations in Geneva and continued by the United Nations. It promotes human, labor, and economic rights around the world.

Office of the High Commissioner for Human Rights *www.ohchr.org*
The High Commissioner title was created in 1993 to bring together under one officer all UN activities relating to human rights. The High Commissioner reports directly to the Secretary–General. The office is based in Geneva and in New York at UN headquarters. Louise Arbour, a former judge in Canada and at the International Court in the The Hague, Netherlands, has been High Commissioner since 2004.

Advocacy NGOs—Non-governmental organizations that promote a specific cause.

Association of Southeast Asian Nations (ASEAN)—A regional attempt to bring Southeast Asia and its enormous population together on behalf of common interests.

Colonialism—The establishment of control of foreign territories.

European Union (EU)—An institutional framework for the construction of an economically, legislatively, judicially, and socially united Europe.

Globalization—The trend to a single, interdependent, and integrated world.

Governance—The act or manner of conducting the policy and operations of an organization.

International Labour Organization (ILO)—A specialized agency of the UN that promotes social justice and internationally recognized human and labor rights.

Non-governmental organization (NGO)—Any not-for-profit agency generally formed around a focused set of goals and having no affiliation with any government or business.

North American Free Trade Agreement (NAFTA)—Trade agreement that encourages free trade between Canada, Mexico, and the United States.

Outsourcing—When businesses move work to a country with lower wages.

Operational NGOs—Non-governmental organizations that implement development projects.

NOTES

1. Quoted by Thomas Friedman in "To Speak to a Young Indian with Aspirations, Press 1," *New York Times* Op Ed column, February 29, 2004.

2. Ibid.

3. This paragraph expands the situation described by Friedman and imagines the process taking place in the classroom.

4. Friedman, "To Speak to a Young Indian with Aspirations, Press 1."

5. Philippe Legrain, *Open World: The Truth about Globalization*. Chicago: Ivan R. Dee, 2004, p.11.

6. Alison Brysk, reworking the definition by Jan Aart Scholte in *Globalization and Human Rights*. Berkeley, CA: University of California Press, 2002, p.6.

7. John Locke, from *Concerning Civil Government,* 1690, quoted by Jack Donnelly, "What Are Human Rights?" Retrieved on May 14, 2004 from http://usinfo.state.gov/products/pubs/hrintro/donnelly.htm, p.1.

8. Ibid., p.1.

9. Ibid., 2.

10. Retrieved on May 14, 2004 from http://usinfo.state.gov/products/pubs/hrintro/declare.htm, 1.

11. Retrieved on May 14, 2004 from http://usinfo/state/gov/products/pubs/hrintro/bill.htm, 1.

12. Donnelly, "What Are Human Rights?" p. 4.

13. Cited in http://www.un.org/aboutun/charter/preamble.htm, p. 1.

14. Cited in http://www.un.org/Overview/rights.html, p. 1.

15. Ibid., p. 4.

16. Ibid., pp. 4–5.

17. Ibid., 5.

18. From Vienna Declaration, section 25. Retrieved on July 18, 2004 from http://www.unhchr.ch/huridocda/huridoca.nsf/(Symbol)/A.CONF.157.23.En?OpenDocument.

19. Ibid., section 74.

20. UN Commission on Human Rights, Sub-commission on the Prevention of Discrimination and Protection of Minorities, Resolution of 4 September 1998, pp.2–3. Retrieved on July 18, 2004 from http://pdhre.org/involved/uncommission.html.

21. Ibid., pp.7–8.

22. Ibid., p. 8.

23. Retrieved on July 17, 2004 from http://www.ilo.org/public/english/wcsdg/docs/report.pdf, p. ix.

24. Ibid., p.x.

25. Ibid., p. xiii.

26. Ibid., p. 13. Italics in original.

27. Ibid., p. 15. Italics in original.

28. Joseph Stiglitz, *Globalization and Its Discontents*. New York: W.W. Norton & Company, 2002, p.81.

29. Ibid., p. 248.

30. Thomas Friedman, *The Lexus and the Olive Tree*. New York: Farrar Straus and Giroux, 1999, p.174.

31. Legrain, *Open World: The Truth about Globalization*, p. 21.

32. Amy Chua, *World on Fire. How Exporting Free Market Democracy Breeds Ethnic Hatred and Global Instability*. New York: Doubleday, 2003, p.259.

33. Friedman, *The Lexus and the Olive Tree,* p. 360.

34. *The New York Times,* May 20, 2004.

35. Om Malik, "The New Land of Opportunity. It's a *Global* Economy— So Quit Whining about Outsourcing. India's Booming Middle Class Has $420 Billion to Spend. Here's How to Grab Your Share," *Business 2.0* (July 2004): 74.

36. Zbigniew Brzezinski, *Global Domination or Global Leadership*. New York: Basic Books, 2004, p.144.

37. Legrain, *Open World: The Truth about Globalization*, p. 21.

38. Ibid., p. 55.

39. Ibid., p. 63.

40. Amy Waldman, "The Saturday Profile. A Young American Outsources Himself," *The New York Times*, July 17, 2004.

41. Ben Stein, "Everybody's Business. The Tale of the Toaster, or How Trade Deficits Are Good," *New York Times*, April 25, 2004.

42. This section is distilled from the author's personal experiences in Poland, 1990 to 2003.

43. Jagdish Bhagwati, *In Defense of Globalization*. New York: Oxford University Press, 2004, p. 76.

44. Ibid., p. 71.

45. Friedman, "To Speak to a Young Indian with Aspirations, Press 1."

46. Legrain, *Open World: The Truth about Globalization*, p. 318.

47. Ibid., p. 297.

48. Retrieved on July 17, 2004 from http://www.ilo.org/public/english/ wcsdg/docs/report.pdf, p. x.

49. Becker, Elizabeth, "UN Study Finds Global Trade Benefits are Uneven," *The New York Times*, February 24, 2004.

50. Retrieved on July 17, 2004 from http://www.ilo.org/public/english/ wcsdg/docs/report.pdf, p. 14.

51. Brysk, *Globalization and Human Rights*, p. 4.

52. Retrieved on July 17, 2004 from http://www.ilo.org/public/english/ wcsdg/docs/report.pdf, p. xii.

53. Brzezinski, *Global Domination or Global Leadership*, p. 172.

54. Legrain, *Open World: The Truth about Globalization*, p. 329.

55. Retrieved on July 18, 2004 from http://www.cdp-hrc.uottawa.ca/ publicat/bull37.html, p. 3.

56. Ibid., p. 4.

57. Ibid., p. 5.

58. Ibid., p. 7.

59. Rifkin, Ira. "Offshore Outsourcing is Moral Issue in Presidential Campaign," *Orlando Sentinel*, March 17, 2004.

60. Brysk, *Globalization and Human Rights*, p. 243.

61. Bhagwati, *In Defense of Globalization*, p. 243.

62. "International Human Rights Day December 10, 2003. In Commemoration. Retrieved on May 14, 2004 from http://www7.nationalacademies.org/ humanrights/Int_Human_Rights_Day _2003.html.

63. Donnelly, "What Are Human Rights?" Retrieved on May 14, 2004 from http://usinfo.state.gov/products/pubs/ hrintro/donnelly.htm, pp. 9–10.

64. Ibid., p.10.

65. Ibid., p.11.

66. Brysk, *Globalization and Human Rights*, p. 246

67. "Categorizing NGOs." Retrieved on July 24, 2004 from http://docs.lib.duke .edu/igo/guides/ngo/define.htm, p. 1.

68. "Milestones in the History of NGOs." Retrieved on July 25, 2004 from http://www.fimcivilsociety.org/english/ MilestonesInTheHistoryOfNGOs.htm.

69. James A. Paul, "NGO Access at the UN," 1999. Retrieved on July 25, 2004 from http://www.globalpolicy .org/ngos/analysis/jap-accs.htm.

70. Bhagwati, *In Defense of Globalization*, p. 36.

71. Ibid., p. 42.

72. Ibid., p. 42.

73. Brysk, *Globalization and Human Rights*, p.246.

74. "Urgent Action Saves Lives: Sign Up Today." Retrieved on July 25, 2004 from http://web.amnesty.org/pages/ ua-index-eng.

75. Retrieved on July 24, 2004 from http://www.derechos.org/human-rights/ lists/.

76. Retrieved on July 24, 2004 from http://www.derechos.org/news/.

77. "About the Center for Religious Freedom." Retrieved on July 25, 2004 from http://www.freedomhouse.org/religion/about/about.htm.

78. Megan Clyne, "Freedom Fighter, *National Review* (December 27, 2004): 27.

79. "About Global Exchange. Program Summary." Retrieved on July 25, 2004 from http://www.globalexchange.org/about/programSummary.html.

80. "About HREA." Retrieved on July 28, 2004 from http://www.hrea.org/abouthrea.html.

81. "HREA Online June/July 2004." Retrieved on July 28, 2004 from http://www.hrea.org/pubs/newsletter/july2004.html.

82. "Human Rights First. About Us." Retrieved on July 25, 2004 from http://www.humanrightsfirst.org/about_us/about_us.htm.

83. Retrieved on July 25, 2004 from http://www.humanrightsfirst.org/about_us/2003_Annual_Report.pdf, p. 6.

84. "Human Rights First. 2004 Awards Dinner." Retrieved on July 25, 2004 from http://www.humanrightsfirst.org/about_us/award_dinners/2004_dinner/2004_dinner.htm.

85. "A Tri-Yearly Publication of HRI." Retrieved on July 25, 2004 from http://www.hri.ca/tribune.

86. "Human Strategies for Human Rights." Retrieved on July 27, 2004 from http://www.hshr.org/background.html.

87. Retrieved on July 24, 2004 from http://www.hshr.org.

88. "About HRW [Human Rights Watch]." Retrieved on July 25, 2004 from http://www.humanrightswatch.org/about/whoweare.html, p.1.

89. "Discover the Red Cross." Retrieved on July 25, 2004 from http://www.icrc.org/Web/Eng/siteeng0.nsf/htmlall/section_discover_the_icrc?OpenDocument.

90. "Strategic Plan." Retrieved on July 28, 2004 from http://www.oxfam.org/eng/about_strat_mission.htm.

91. "What We Do." Retrieved on July 28, 2004 from http://www.oxfam.org/eng/about_what.htm.

92. "What We Do." Retrieved on July 28, 2004 from http://www.oxfam.org/eng/about_what.htm.

93. Tony Vento, "Projects of the Heart," in Mike Prokosch and Laura Raymond, eds., *The Global Activist's Manual. Local Ways to Change the World.* New York: Thunder's Mouth Press/Nation Books, 2002, p. 218.

94. Ibid., pp. 218–19.

95. Ibid., p. 219.

96. Indian NGOs. "People's Forum." Retrieved on July 27, 2004 from http://www.indianngos.com/people/schwab/jeroo.htm.

97. Robert Bornstein, *How to Change the World. Social Entrepreneurs and the Power of New Ideas.* New York: Oxford University Press, Inc., 2004, p. 89.

98. Ibid., p. 88.

99. Thomas Friedman, "Origin of Species," *The New York Times,* March 14, 2004.

100. Friedman, "Origin of Species."

101. Zbigniew Brzezinski, *The Choice: Global Domination or Global Leadership.* New York: Basic Books, 2004, p. ix.

102. Ibid., p. xi.

103. Friedman, *The Lexus and the Olive* Tree, p. 310.

104. Brzezinski, *The Choice: Global Domination or Global Leadership*, pp. 186–89.

105. Ibid., pp. 186–87.

106. Ibid., p. 187.

107. Ibid., p. 142.

108. Bhagwati, *In Defense of Globalization*, p. 249.

109. Ibid., p. 249.

110. Ibid., p. 250.

111. Ibid., p. 251.

112. Ibid., p. 252.

113. United States Institute of Peace. "About Us." Retrieved on July 30, 2004 from http://www.usip.org/aboutus/index.html, p.1

114. "Advancing Human Rights and Peace in a Complex World." Retrieved from http://www.usip.org/pubs/specialreports/sr86.html on May 14, 2004, p.13.

115. Ibid., p. 7.

116. Ibid., p. 7.

117. Ibid., p. 8.

118. Donnelly, "What Are Human Rights?"p.12.

119. Fourth World Conference on Women Beijing Declaration. Retrieved on August 1, 2004 from http://www.un.org/womenwatch/daw/beijing/platform/declar.htm, p.2.

120. Ibid., p. 5.

121. Ibid., p. 5–6.

122. Bhagwati, *In Defense of Globalization*, p. 89.

123. Ibid.

124. Brysk, *Globalization and Human Rights*, p. 243.

125. Bhagwati, *In Defense of Globalization*, p. 69.

126. Ibid., p. 70.

127. Ibid., p. 71.

128. Legrain, *Open World: The Truth about Globalization*, p. 63.

129. Kathie Lee Gifford and Sweat Shop Allegations. Retrieved April 19, 2005 from http://www.american.edu/TED/kathylee.htm.

130. "Four Chains Bought from Sweatshops that Exploit Workers." Retrieved on August 1, 2004 from http://www.cnn.com/US/9712/14/sweatshop.retailers/.

131. Liedtke, Michael. "Gap to Help Workers. U.S. Garment Retailer Takes Aim at 'Sweatshops,'" *Orlando Sentinel*, May 13, 2004, C3.

132. Ibid.

133. Legrain, *Open World: The Truth about Globalization*, p. 63.

134. "Fact Sheet #17. Committee against Torture." Retrieved on August 1, 2004 from http://www.unhchr.ch/html/menu6/2/fs17.htm.

135. Rosenberg, Tina. "John Kamm's Third Way." *The New York Times Sunday Magazine*, March 3, 2002. Retrieved on August 1, 2004 from http://www.duihua.org/press/media/nyt_article.htm, p.1.

136. Ibid., p. 2.

137. "Advancing Human Rights and Peace in a Complex World." Retrieved from http://www.usip.org/pubs/specialreports/sr86.html on May 14, 2004, p.10.

138. Ibid., p. 9.

139. "BSR History." Retrieved on August 1, 2004 from http://www.bsr.org/Meta/about/BSRHistory.cfm, p.1.

140. "Human Rights." Business for Social Responsibility. Retrieved on August 1, 2004 from http://www.bsr.org/AdvisoryServices/HumanRights.cfm, p. 2.

141. Thomas Friedman, "Software of Democracy," *The New York Times*, March 21, 2004.

142. Thomas Friedman, "Think Global, Act Local," *The New York Times*, June 6, 2004.

143. Brysk, *Globalization and Human Rights*, p. 243.

144. Brysk, *Globalization and Human Rights*, p. 245.

145. Edward Rothstein "Globalize Soccer? Not in Your Lifetime, Chum," *The New York Times*, June 26, 2004.

146. Donnelly, "What Are Human Rights?" p. 8.

147. Quoted by Warren Hoge in "The Saturday Profile. Rescuing Victims Worldwide 'From the Depths of Hell,'" *The New York Times*, July 10, 2004.

BOOKS AND ARTICLES

"2003 Annual Report." Human Rights First. Retrieved on July 25, 2004 from http://www.humanrightsfirst.org/about_us/2003_Annual_Report.pdf, p.6.

"2004 Awards Dinner." Human Rights First. Retrieved on July 25, 2004 fromhttp://www.humanrightsfirst.org/about_us/award_dinners/ 2004_dinner/2004_dinner.htm.

"A Fair Globalization: Creating Opportunities for All." ILO Report from World Commission on the Social Dimension of Globalization published February 2004. Retrieved on July 17, 2004 fromhttp://www.ilo.org/ public/english/wcsdg/docs/report.pdf.

"A tri-yearly publication of HRI [Human Rights International]." Retrieved on July 25, 2004 from http://www.hri.ca/tribune/.

About Al Jazeera. Retrieved on February 9, 2005 from http://english.aljazeera.net/ NR/exeres/5D7F956E-6B52-46D9-8D17-448856D01CDB.htm.

"About BSR [Business for Social Responsibility]." Retrieved on August 1, 2004 from http://www.bsr.org/Meta/About/index.cfm.

"About the Center for Religious Freedom." Retrieved on July 25, 2004 from http://www.freedomhouse.org/religion/about/about.htm.

"About Global Exchange. Program Summary." Retrieved on July 25, 2004 from http://www.globalexchange.org/about/programSummary.html.

"About HREA [Human Rights Education Associates]." Retrieved on July 28, 2004 from http://www.hrea.org/abouthrea.html.

"About HRW [Human Rights Watch]." Retrieved on July 25, 2004 from http://www.humanrightswatch.org/about/whoweare.html.

"About Us." Human Rights First. Retrieved on July 25, 2004 from http://www.humanrightsfirst.org/about_us/about_us.htm.

"About Us." Oxfam International. Retrieved on July 28, 2004 from http://www.oxfam.org/eng/about.htm.

"About Us." TransFair USA. Retrieved on July 27, 2004 from http://www.transfairusa.org/content/about/aboutus.php.

"About Us." United States Institute of Peace. Retrieved on July 30, 2004 from http://www.usip.org/aboutus/index.html.

"Advancing Human Rights and Peace in a Complex World." Retrieved on May 14, 2004 from http://www.usip.org/pubs/specialreports/sr86.html.

Becker, Elizabeth. "UN Study Finds Global Trade Benefits are Uneven." *The New York Times,* February 24, 2004.

Bhagwati, Jagdish. *In Defense of Globalization.* New York: Oxford University Press, Inc., 2004.

The Bill of Rights. Retrieved on May 14, 2004 from http://usinfo/state/gov/products/pubs/hrintro/bill.htm.

Bornstein, David. *How to Change the World. Social Entrepreneurs and the Power of New Ideas.* New York: Oxford University Press, Inc., 2004.

Brady, Thomas J. "'Open World' Details the Economic Benefits of Globalization." *Orlando Sentinel,* April 18, 2004.

Brysk, Alison, ed. *Globalization and Human Rights.* Berkeley, CA: University of California Press, 2002.

Brzezinski, Zbigniew. *The Choice. Global Domination or Global Leadership.* New York: Basic Books, 2004.

"BSR [Business for Social Responsibility] History." Retrieved on August 1, 2004 from http://www.bsr.org/Meta/about/BSRHistory.cfm.

"Categorizing NGOs." Retrieved on July 24, 2004 from http://docs.lib.duke.edu/igo/guides/ngo/define.htm.

Chua, Amy. *World on Fire. How Exporting Free Market Democracy Breeds Ethnic Hatred and Global Instability.* New York: Doubleday, 2003.

Clyne, Meghan. "Freedom Fighter. Meet the 'Very Focused, and Tough' Nina Shea." *National Review* December 27, 2004: 27.

Dalai Lama. "Humanity and Globalization: Human Rights on the Eve of the 21st Century," Speech on December 8, 1998. Retrieved on July 18, 2004 from http://www.cdphrc.uottawa.ca/publicat/bull37.html.

"Discover the Red Cross." Retrieved on July 25, 2004 from http://www.icrc.org/ Web/Eng/siteeng0.nsf/htmlall/section_discover_the_icrc?OpenDocument.

Donnelly, Jack. "What are Human Rights?" Retrieved on May 14, 2004 from http://usinfo.state.gov/products/pubs/hrintro/donnelly.htm.

Drezner, Daniel W. "Globalization without Riots. An India-Born British-Educated American Tries to Calm the Streets." *The New York Times Book Review*, April 18, 2004.

"The Dui Hua Foundation." Retrieved on August 1, 2004 from http://www.duihua.org/.

"Fact Sheet #17. Committee against Torture." Retrieved on August 1, 2004 from http://www.unhchr.ch/html/menu6/2/fs17.htm.

"Fair Trade Overview." TransFair USA. Retrieved on July 27, 2004 from http://www.transfairusa.org/content/about/overview.php.

"Four Chains Bought from Sweatshops that Exploit Workers." Retrieved on August 1, 2004 from http://www.cnn.com/US/9712/14/ sweatshop.retailers/.

Fourth World Conference on Women Beijing Declaration. Retrieved on August 1, 2004 from http://www.un.org/womenwatch/daw/beijing/ platform/declar.htm.

Friedman, Thomas L. *The Lexus and the Olive Tree. Understanding Globalization.* New York: Farrar, Straus, and Giroux, 1999.

———. "Making India Shine," The *New York Times,* May 20, 2004.

———. "Origin of Species," The *New York Times,* March 14, 2004.

———. "Software of Democracy," The *New York Times,* March 21, 2004.

———. "Think Global, Act Local," The *New York Times,* June 6, 2004.

———. "To Speak to a Young Indian with Aspirations, Press 1. The Story of 30 Little Turtles." The *New York Times,* February 29, 2004.

Hoge, Warren. "The Saturday Profile. Rescuing Victims Worldwide 'From the Depths of Hell.'" The *New York Times,* July 10, 2004.

Holstein, William J. "Book Value: Of Globalization and the Greater Good." *The New York Times,* February 22, 2004.

"HREA [Human Rights Education Associates] Online June/July 2004." Retrieved on July 28, 2004 from http://www.hrea.org/pubs/newsletter/july2004.html.

"Human Rights." Retrieved on May 15, 2004 from http://www.un.org/Depts/dhl/resguide/spechr.htm.

"Human Rights." Business for Social Responsibility. Retrieved on August 1, 2004 from http://www.bsr.org/Advisory Services/HumanRights.cfm.

"Human Rights Mailing Lists." Derechos Human Rights. Retrieved on July 24, 2004 from http://www.derechos.org/human-rights/lists/.

"Human Rights News & Actions." Derechos Human Rights. Retrieved on July 24, 2004 from http://www.derechos.org/news/.

"Human Rights Organizations & Resources." Retrieved on May 14, 2004 from http://www.hrweb.org/resource.html.

Human Strategies for Human Rights. Retrieved on July 27, 2004 from http://www.hshr.org/background.html.

Human Strategies for Human Rights. Retrieved on July 24, 2004 from http://www.hshr.org.

Jefferson, Thomas. "The Declaration of Independence." Retrieved on May 14, 2004 from http://usinfo.state.gov/products/pubs/hrintro/declare.htm.

Kathie Lee Gifford and Sweat Shop Allegations. Retrieved on April 19, 2005 from http://www.american.edu/TED/kathylee.htm.

Legrain, Philippe. *Open World: The Truth about Globalization.* Chicago: Ivan R. Dee, 2004.

Liedtke, Michael. "Gap to Help Workers. U.S. Garment Retailer Takes Aim at 'Sweatshops.'" *Orlando Sentinel* (May 13, 2004): C3.

Malik, Om. "The New Land of Opportunity. It's a *Global* Economy—So Quit Whining about Outsourcing. India's Booming Middle Class Has $420 Billion to Spend. Here's How to Grab Your Share." *Business 2.0* (July 2004): pp.72–79.

"Milestones in the History of NGOs." Retrieved on July 25, 2004 from http://www.fimcivilsociety.org/english/MilestonesInTheHistory OfNGOs.htm.

Paul, James A. "NGO Access at the UN." Updated July1999. Retrieved on July 25, 2004 from http://www.globalpolicy.org/ngos/analysis/ jap-accs.htm.

"People's Forum." Indian NGOs. Retrieved on July 27, 2004 from http://www.indianngos.com/people/schwab/jeroo.htm.

Pitts, David. "Human Rights Watch." Retrieved on May 14, 2004 from http://usinfo.state.gov/products/pubs/hrintro/watch.htm.

Preamble to UN Charter. Retrieved on May 15, 2004 from http://un.org/ aboutun/charter/preamble.htm.

Rifkin, Ira. "Offshore Outsourcing is Moral Issue in Presidential Campaign." *Orlando Sentinel,* March 17, 2004.

Rosenberg, Tina. "John Kamm's Third Way." *The New York Times Sunday Magazine,* March 3, 2002. Retrieved on August 1, 2004 from http://www.duihua.org/press/media/nyt_article.htm.

Rothstein, Edward. "Globalize Soccer? Not in Your Lifetime, Chum." *The New York Times,* June 26, 2004.

"Shirin Ebadi." Retrieved on July 23, 2004 from http://almaz.com/nobel/ peace/2003a.html.

"Shirin Ebadi," Retrieved on July 23, 2004 from http://www.hrw.org/ press/2003/10/ebadi-bio.htm.

Stein, Ben. "Everybody's Business. The Tale of the Toaster, or How Trade Deficits are Good." *New York Times,* April 25, 2004.

Stiglitz, Joseph E. *Globalization and Its Discontents.* New York: W.W. Norton & Company, 2002.

"Strategic Plan." Oxfam International. Retrieved on July 28, 2004 from http://www.oxfam.org/eng/about_strat_mission.htm.

UN Commission on Human Rights Resolutions of September 4, 1998 and August 26, 1999. Retrieved on July 18, 2004 from http://pdhre.org/involved/uncommission.html.

Universal Declaration of Human Rights. Retrieved on May 15, 2004 from http://www.un.org/Overview/rights.html.

"Urgent Action Saves Lives: sign up today." Retrieved on July 25, 2004 from http://web.amnesty.org/pages/ua-index-eng.

Vento, Tony. "Projects of the Heart," *The Global Activist's Manual. Local Ways to Change the World.* Prokosch, Mike and Laura Raymond, eds. New York: Thunder's Mouth Press/Nation Books, 2002.

Vienna Declaration on Human Rights. Retrieved on July 18, 2004 from http://www.unhchr.ch/huridocda/huridoca.nsf/(Symbol)/A.CONF.157.23.En?OpenDocument.

Waldman, Amy. "Indians Go Home, but Don't Leave U.S. Behind." The *New York Times* (July 24, 2004), p.1.

———. "The Saturday Profile. A Young American Outsources Himself." The *New York Times,* July 17, 2004.

Walker, Rob. "Brewed Awakening? Coffee Beans, Globalization and the Branding of Ethics." *New York Times Magazine,* June 6, 2004.

"Welcome to Freedom House." Retrieved on July 28, 2004 from http://www.freedomhouse.org/.

"What We Do." Oxfam International. Retrieved on July 28, 2004 from http://www.oxfam.org/eng/about_what.htm.

"Who We Are." TransFair USA. Retrieved on July 27, 2004 from http://www.transfairusa.org/content/about/whoeare.php.

Wiesel, Torsten. "International Human Rights Day December 10, 2003. In Commemoration. Retrieved on May 14, 2004 from http://www7.nationalacademies.org/humanrights/Int_Human_Rights_Day_2003.html.

BOOKS

Bhagwati, Jagdish. *In Defense of Globalization.* New York: Oxford University Press, 2004.

Bornstein, David. *How to Change the World.* New York: Oxford University Press, 2004.

Brzezinski, Zbigniew. *The Choice: Global Domination or Global Leadership.* New York: Basic Books, 2004.

Chua, Amy. *The World on Fire: How Exporting Free Market Democracy Breeds Ethnic Hatred and Global Instability.* New York: Doubleday, 2003.

Friedman, Thomas L. *The Lexus and the Olive Tree. Understanding Globalization.* New York: Farrar, Straus, and Giroux, 1999.

Legrain, Philippe. *Open World: The Truth about Globalization.* Chicago: Ivan R. Dee, 2004.

INDEX

PICTURE CREDITS

Alma Kadragic earned a Ph.D. in English literature, because in her family a doctorate was as natural as devouring books and speaking several languages. She taught English literature and composition at the City University of New York as a graduate student and went on to a career in broadcast journalism. She spent 16 years with ABC News at the network level in New York, Washington, D.C., London, and Warsaw as writer, producer, and bureau chief.

In 1990, Kadragic left ABC to run her own business, Alcat Communications International, Inc, a public relations and marketing company working primarily in Poland and Central Europe until 2003. During that time she cofounded the Polish PR Association and coauthored the first public relations handbook in Polish.

Now she runs Alcat from a home office in Winter Park, Florida, and works with corporate clients as a consultant and writer, producing everything from speeches to strategic and marketing plans, annual reports, and economic impact reports. She also writes columns and articles on entrepreneurship, business, marketing, and multicultural communications for newspapers and magazines.

Kadragic returned to college teaching in 2003, offering courses in English, speech, and broadcast news at Seminole Community College and the University of Central Florida. Since 2004, she has been teaching communications courses at the University of Phoenix in Orlando and online.

James Bacchus is Chairman of the Global Trade Practice Group of the international law firm Greenberg Traurig, Professional Association. He is also a visiting professor of international law at Vanderbilt University Law School. He served previously as a special assistant to the United States Trade Representative; as a Member of the Congress of the United States, from Florida; and as a Member, for eight years, and Chairman, for two terms, of the Appellate Body of the World Trade Organization. His book, *Trade and Freedom*, was published by Cameron May in London in 2004, and is now in its third edition worldwide.

Ilan Alon, Ph.D, is Associate Professor of International Business at the Crummer Graduate School of Business of Rollins College. He holds a Ph.D in International Business and Economics from Kent State University. He currently teaches courses on Business in the Global Environment and Emerging Markets: China in the business curriculum as well as International Trade and Economics in the economics curriculum.